Drugs, Crime, and Criminal Justice

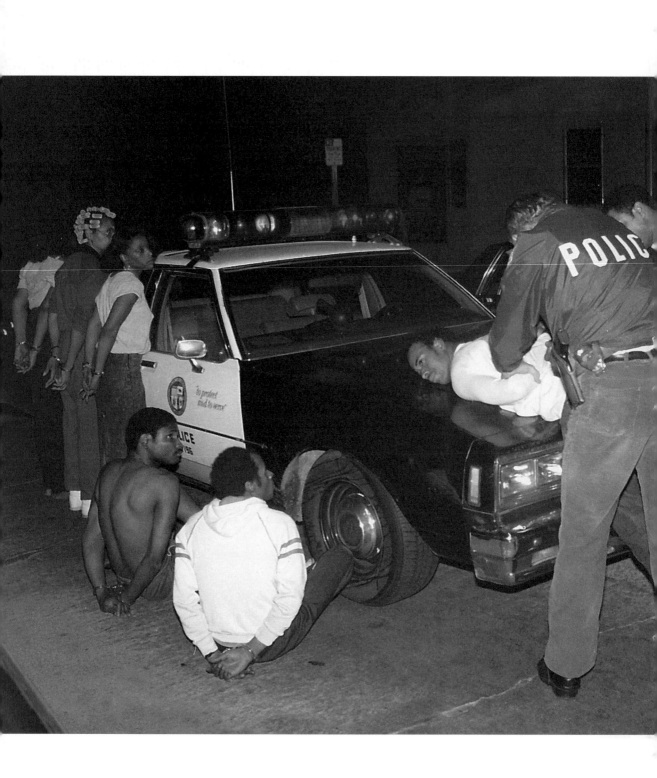

CRIME, JUSTICE, AND PUNISHMENT

Drugs, Crime, and Criminal Justice

Linda Bayer

Austin Sarat, GENERAL EDITOR

CHELSEA HOUSE PUBLISHERS
Philadelphia

Frontispiece: *Los Angeles police officers arrest suspects during a drug sweep.*

Produced by 21st Century Publishing and Communications, Inc., New York, N.Y.

Chelsea House Publishers

Editor in Chief Sally Cheney
Associate Editor in Chief Kim Shinners
Production Manager Pamela Loos
Art Director Sara Davis
Director of Photography Judy L. Hasday
Cover Designer Keith Trego

First Printing

1 3 5 7 9 8 6 4 2

The Chelsea House World Wide Web address is
http://www.chelseahouse.com

Library of Congress Cataloging-in-Publication Data

Bayer, Linda N.
Drugs, crime, and criminal justice / Linda Bayer;
Austin Sarat, general editor.
  p. cm. — (Crime, justice, and punishment)
Includes bibliographical references and index.

ISBN 0-7910-4262-6

1. Drug abuse and crime—United States—Juvenile
literature. 2. Narcotics, Control of—United States—
Juvenile literature. 3. Criminal justice, Administration
of—United States—Juvenile literature. [1. Drug abuse
and crime. 2. Narcotics, Control of. 3. Criminal
justice, Administration of.] I. Sarat, Austin. II. Title.
III. Series.

HV5825.B393 2001
364.2'4—dc21

2001028521

Contents

Fears and Fascinations:

An Introduction to Crime,
Justice, and Punishment
Austin Sarat   7

1   Why Drugs Are Illegal   13

2   America's Early Drug History   21

3   Changing Viewpoints   33

4   The Drug-Crime Connection   45

5   Drug Policy and Criminal Justice   51

6   Rehab Behind Bars?   61

7   Rights Versus Protection   69

8   International Drug Trafficking   81

9   A Look at the Future   95

Further Reading   106
Index   108

CRIME, JUSTICE, AND PUNISHMENT

CAPITAL PUNISHMENT

CHILDREN, VIOLENCE, AND MURDER

CLASSIC CONS AND SWINDLES

CRIMES AGAINST CHILDREN:
CHILD ABUSE AND NEGLECT

CRIMES AGAINST HUMANITY

CYBER CRIMES

DEFENSE LAWYERS

DRUGS, CRIME,
AND CRIMINAL JUSTICE

THE DUTY TO RESCUE

ESPIONAGE AND TREASON

THE FBI

THE FBI'S MOST WANTED

FORENSIC SCIENCE

GANGS AND CRIME

THE GRAND JURY

GREAT PROSECUTIONS

GREAT ROBBERIES

GUNS, CRIME, AND
THE SECOND AMENDMENT

HATE CRIMES

HIGH CRIMES AND MISDEMEANORS:
THE IMPEACHMENT PROCESS

INFAMOUS TRIALS

THE INSANITY DEFENSE

JUDGES AND SENTENCING

THE JURY SYSTEM

JUVENILE CRIME

MAJOR UNSOLVED CRIMES

ORGANIZED CRIME

PRISONS

PRIVATE INVESTIGATORS
AND BOUNTY HUNTERS

PUNISHMENT AND REHABILITATION

RACE, CRIME, AND PUNISHMENT

REVENGE AND RETRIBUTION

RIGHTS OF THE ACCUSED

SERIAL MURDER

TERRORISM

VICTIMS AND VICTIMS' RIGHTS

WHITE-COLLAR CRIME

Fears and Fascinations:

An Introduction to
Crime, Justice, and Punishment

By Austin Sarat

We live with crime and images of crime all around us. Crime evokes in most of us a deep aversion, a feeling of profound vulnerability, but it also evokes an equally deep fascination. Today, in major American cities the fear of crime is a major fact of life, some would say a disproportionate response to the realities of crime. Yet the fear of crime is real, palpable in the quickened steps and furtive glances of people walking down darkened streets. At the same time, we eagerly follow crime stories on television and in movies. We watch with a "who done it" curiosity, eager to see the illicit deed done, the investigation undertaken, the miscreant brought to justice and given his just deserts. On the streets the presence of crime is a reminder of our own vulnerability and the precariousness of our taken-for-granted rights and freedoms. On television and in the movies the crime story gives us a chance to probe our own darker motives, to ask "Is there a criminal within?" as well as to feel the collective satisfaction of seeing justice done.

Fear and fascination, these two poles of our engagement with crime, are, of course, only part of the story. Crime is, after all, a major social and legal problem, not just an issue of our individual psychology. Politicians today use our fear of, and fascination with, crime for political advantage. How we respond to crime, as well as to the political uses of the crime issue, tells us a lot about who we are as a people as well as what we value and what we tolerate. Is our response compassionate or severe? Do we seek to understand or to punish, to enact an angry vengeance or to rehabilitate and welcome the criminal back into our midst? The CRIME, JUSTICE, AND PUNISHMENT series is designed to explore these themes, to ask why we are fearful and fascinated, to probe the meanings and motivations of crimes and criminals and of our responses to them, and, finally, to ask what we can learn about ourselves and the society in which we live by examining our responses to crime.

Crime is always a challenge to the prevailing normative order and a test of the values and commitments of law-abiding people. It is sometimes a Raskolnikov-like act of defiance, an assertion of the unwillingness of some to live according to the rules of conduct laid out by organized society. In this sense, crime marks the limits of the law and reminds us of law's all-too-regular failures. Yet sometimes there is more desperation than defiance in criminal acts; sometimes they signal a deep pathology or need in the criminal. To confront crime is thus also to come face-to-face with the reality of social difference, of class privilege and extreme deprivation, of race and racism, of children neglected, abandoned, or abused whose response is to enact on others what they have experienced themselves. And occasionally crime, or what is labeled a criminal act, represents a call for justice, an appeal to a higher moral order against the inadequacies of existing law.

Figuring out the meaning of crime and the motivations of criminals and whether crime arises from defiance, desperation, or the appeal for justice is never an easy task. The motivations and meanings of crime are as varied as are the persons who engage in criminal conduct. They are as mysterious as any of the mysteries of the human soul. Yet the desire to know the secrets of crime and the criminal is a strong one, for in that knowledge may lie one step on the road to protection, if not an assurance of one's own personal safety. Nonetheless, as strong as that desire may be, there is no available technology that can allow us to know the whys of crime with much confidence, let alone a scientific certainty. We can, however, capture something about crime by studying the defiance, desperation, and quest for justice that may be associated with it. Books in the Crime, Justice, and Punishment series will take up that challenge. They tell stories of crime and criminals, some famous, most not, some glamorous and exciting, most mundane and commonplace.

This series will, in addition, take a sober look at American criminal justice, at the procedures through which we investigate crimes and identify criminals, at the institutions in which innocence or guilt is determined. In these procedures and institutions we confront the thrill of the chase as well as the challenge of protecting the rights of those who defy our laws. It is through the efficiency and dedication of law enforcement that we might capture the criminal; it is in the rare instances of their corruption or brutality that we feel perhaps our deepest betrayal. Police, prosecutors, defense lawyers, judges, and jurors administer criminal justice and in their daily actions give substance to the guarantees of the Bill of Rights. What is an adversarial system of justice? How does it work? Why do we have it? Books in the Crime, Justice, and Punishment series will examine the thrill of the chase as we seek to capture the criminal. They will also reveal the drama and majesty of the criminal trial as well as the day-to-day reality of a criminal justice system in which trials are the exception and negotiated pleas of guilty are the rule.

When the trial is over or the plea has been entered, when we have separated the innocent from the guilty, the moment of punishment has arrived. The injunction to punish the guilty, to respond to pain inflicted by inflicting pain, is as old as civilization itself. "An eye for an eye and a tooth for a tooth" is a biblical reminder that punishment must measure pain for pain. But our response to the criminal must be better than and different from the crime itself. The biblical admonition, along with the constitutional prohibition of "cruel and unusual punishment," signals that we seek to punish justly and to be just not only in the determination of who can and should be punished, but in how we punish as well. But neither reminder tells us what to do with the wrongdoer. Do we rape the rapist, or burn the home of the arsonist? Surely justice and decency say no. But, if not, then how can and should we punish? In a world in which punishment is neither identical to the crime nor an automatic response to it, choices must be made and we must make them. Books in the CRIME, JUSTICE, AND PUNISHMENT series will examine those choices and the practices, and politics, of punishment. How do we punish and why do we punish as we do? What can we learn about the rationality and appropriateness of today's responses to crime by examining our past and its responses? What works? Is there, and can there be, a just measure of pain?

CRIME, JUSTICE, AND PUNISHMENT brings together books on some of the great themes of human social life. The books in this series capture our fear and fascination with crime and examine our responses to it. They remind us of the deadly seriousness of these subjects. They bring together themes in law, literature, and popular culture to challenge us to think again, to think anew, about subjects that go to the heart of who we are and how we can and will live together.

*   *   *   *   *

Drugs are today one of the most important and controversial concerns of the criminal justice system. For some the prohibition of drug usage and the severe punishment of those who abuse drugs are central elements of a strategy of effective law enforcement. For others the criminalization of drugs is a vast mistake, diverting resources, imposing costs, dividing our society. Whatever one's perspective on the drug problem and the right way to deal with it, *Drugs, Crime, and Criminal Justice* will be an invaluable resource.

This book provides an interesting, comprehensive account of the criminalization of drugs and its consequences. It has a distinctive perspective and is chock-a-block full of information. From a broad historical overview of the drug problem, it moves to a careful account of the connection between drugs and crime. In addition, it takes its readers behind prison walls to inquire about the impact drugs have on our systems of punishment. Finally, it illuminates the international dimensions of the drug problem and explores various alternatives to current approaches to dealing with the problem. Throughout, *Drugs, Crime, and Criminal Justice* explores the way drugs have been, and will be, an important influence on crime, justice, and punishment in the United States and other nations.

WHY DRUGS
ARE ILLEGAL

L ate one Saturday night, 16-year-old Craig Shapiro lay on his bed with his heart pounding. Several hours before, he had snorted two lines of cocaine, and for a while he had felt both excited and happy—but the feeling was fading. Now he was sweating and sick to his stomach, and he couldn't stop grinding his teeth together. His nose was running, and sharp pains shot through his body. He staggered to his feet and laid out the rest of his cocaine supply in lines on a mirror. Then he used a straw to suck the powder up into his nose.

Once again, a rush of exhilaration spread through his body, and he heaved a sigh of relief. Then he noticed that his chest was still jumping, as though something was trying to get out of his rib cage. As his heart pounded harder and harder, he began to be scared. Pain shot down his arm, and now he promised he would never do drugs again if God would only keep him from dying. If he died he would never know if his

As this drug user cuts a line of cocaine, she not only endangers her physical and emotional well-being but also commits a crime.

13

basketball team went on to the championships . . . he would never get to know Lisa Evans better . . . he would never graduate . . . never have a chance to make up his mind whether he wanted to be a doctor or a pro basketball player. . . .

The pain in his chest grew sharper. Then everything went black.

Fortunately, Craig's mother found him in time. She called an ambulance, and he was rushed to an emergency room. The doctors found he had suffered a heart attack, caused by the cocaine he had ingested. They were able to save his life. Craig was lucky—this time.

If Craig Shapiro *had* died that night, his death would not have made the headlines in the newspapers; no newscasters would have discussed it on the national evening news; and only his family and friends would have been changed forever by his death. The rest of the world would have gone on as usual, because Craig's death would have been just another statistic. He would have been one of the 14,000 people who lose their lives because of drugs every year.

When stars like Jimi Hendrix, Janis Joplin, Elvis Presley, and John Belushi die because of drugs, however, the world takes notice. Partly as a result of these celebrities' deaths, society learned about the dangers of illegal drug use. The U.S. government tightened its drug laws while launching an educational campaign to teach people that drugs are deadly.

Perhaps partly because of this campaign, drug use has dropped dramatically in the United States over the past two decades. In 1979, more than 25 million Americans were using illegal drugs; in 1996, that number had fallen by 12 million. In 1979, 14.1 percent of Americans surveyed had used an illegal drug within the previous month, but in 1997, only 6.1 percent had—a reduction of over 60 percent.

These numbers are encouraging, but unfortunately, the picture isn't completely rosy. In the last few years,

drug use has again begun to increase slightly. According to the U.S. Drug Enforcement Administration (DEA), 13 million Americans used drugs in 1996, but in 1999 that number had increased to almost 15 million. Furthermore, some of the drugs being used today are far stronger than they were in the past. For instance, the average THC (the psychoactive ingredient) content in marijuana in the 1970s was 1.5 percent, while today it averages 7.6 percent. Likewise, heroin's purity levels once ranged from 1 to 10 percent, but today the average purity of heroin is 35 percent. South American heroin, which is available in many East Coast cities, ranges from 70 to 80 percent purity.

The U.S. DEA points to another disturbing trend as well: kids are using drugs more than they did before. According to a survey conducted by the National Center on Addiction and Substance Use, teen marijuana

Every year thousands of people are rushed to the emergency room because of drug overdoses, and 14,000 people will lose their lives because of drugs.

When Elvis Presley, the famous rock idol, died of an apparent heart attack at the age of 42, coroners found traces of at least 10 prescription drugs in his bloodstream.

use has risen by almost 300 percent just since 1992. Between 1991 and 1999, drug use among 13- and 14-year-olds increased by 51 percent. In other words, young people are trying drugs at younger ages—and they are also using more kinds of illegal substances. Drugs like cocaine, heroin, methamphetamines, and marijuana have found their way into schools all over America. Adolescents like Craig Shapiro may pay for this trend with their lives.

Although the consequences of drug abuse are serious, young people continue to experiment with illegal substances. Kids try drugs for a variety of reasons: because they're curious or their friends want them to;

because they're bored or they want to have fun; because they enjoy taking risks or they're unhappy and want to escape from their troubles. Eventually, however, many kids continue to use drugs simply because they are addicted. At this point, their bodies or emotions are dependent on the way drugs make them feel; without drugs they feel sick and anxious.

Not only do the kids who use drugs suffer the consequences, but the cost of illegal drug use in America is a high one in many other ways. We lose the lives and potential of many young adults, and everyone in the United States pays the price for drug use at many levels.

All too often, drugs damage the central core of American society—the family. According to the Office of National Drug Control Policy (ONDCP), drug use causes violence and abuse within families. The ONDCP reported that one-quarter to one-half of all domestic violence is drug-related; substance abuse is a key problem for 81 percent of all families reported for child abuse; and many pregnant women—nearly 80,000—use drugs regularly, causing harm to their unborn children.

Teen Drug Use

Although an alarming number of kids use drugs, this doesn't mean that *most* young people have a drug problem. In fact, many have never even experimented with an illegal substance. One study of high school seniors, reported by George Beschner and Alfred S. Friedman in their book *Teen Drug Use*, found the following percentages (the total is more than 100 percent because many of the students who had tried drugs had tried several different kinds):

- 27 percent had used stimulants.
- 16 percent had used cocaine.
- 15 percent had used hallucinogens, including LSD and PCP.
- 14 percent had used sedatives or barbiturates.
- 14 percent had used inhalants.
- 13 percent had used tranquilizers.
- 10 percent had used opiates other than heroin.
- 9 percent had used LSD.

Drug use also creates a less productive, less safe workplace. A survey conducted by the Substance Abuse and Mental Health Services Administration found that, compared with employees who don't test positive for drugs, employees who do make more than twice as many workers' compensation claims, use almost twice the medical benefits, and take one-third more sick time. Drug users are also 60 percent more likely to cause accidents on the job. The ONDCP estimates that illegal drug use costs American society $110 billion each year.

Drug-related crime accounts for part of this cost, since illegal drug use often leads to other forms of criminal behavior. Many people who commit robbery and engage in prostitution do so in order to get money for drugs. Furthermore, drug use breaks down relationships and destroys inhibitions, thus contributing to crimes of violence. In a book by Ari Kiev called *The Drug Epidemic*, a teenager describes his experiences with drugs and crime:

> I mugged a lady. . . . The only thing I was thinking about was getting that pocketbook, getting her to shut up, running and going out and copping [buying drugs]. . . . I have committed a lot of crimes to get money for drugs. I might have hurt people, I might have done it three or four times a month, rob a store or something. Might have beat people for them. I might have committed these crimes, 'cause all I had in my mind was get the money. My mind was a twenty-four-hour round-the-clock thing—dope, heroin. I must get some heroin for myself. I didn't really care about nobody.

More than half the people who commit crimes in the United States were on drugs at the time they broke the law, and the criminal justice system and American prisons are crowded with drug users. What's more, many drug users are juveniles. In 1994 juvenile courts handled about 120,000 cases that involved drugs, including the possession or sale of marijuana, cocaine, and other illegal substances.

Juveniles who use drugs are also more likely to be involved in violent crimes.

Drug-related crime costs America billions of dollars annually; drug abuse leads to incidents of violence and death in American schools and neighborhoods. Drugs threaten human lives; they threaten the future of the United States. American laws are designed to protect society—and that's why the use of dangerous drugs *is* a crime.

But it wasn't always that way. Believe or not, many drugs—including heroin—were once legal in the United States.

AMERICA'S EARLY DRUG HISTORY

If you had a cough in the 18th century, your doctor might have suggested you dose yourself with the following medication: a teacupful of opium syrup three or four times a day. Or, if you suffered from headaches, he would likely have prescribed an opium powder. Although opium is the substance used to produce heroin, these medicines were all perfectly legal in the 1700s. Opium was marketed under a variety of labels such as: Ayer's Cherry Pectoral, Mrs. Winslow's Soothing Syrup, Godfrey's Cordial, Hamlin's Wizard Oil, and Dover's Powder.

These remedies were advertised as "painkillers," "cough mixtures," "soothing syrups," and "women's friends." They were used to treat everyone from rheumatic grandparents to teething babies. The medicine was thought to cure diarrhea, colds, cholera, fever, cancer, baldness, and athlete's foot. The medicine may have soothed the patients' pain for a short period of time, but many people, including babies, suffered

These Afghan farmers are harvesting raw opium from poppy heads. In the 18th and 19th centuries, opium was not illegal in the United States, and many Americans used it regularly for various purposes.

21

addiction, withdrawal pains, and even death.

By the 19th century, Americans were also using morphine, another drug derived from opium. The invention of the hypodermic syringe allowed this medication to be injected directly into the bloodstream, and its use as a painkiller became common during the Civil War. According to the *Encyclopaedia Britannica,* this practice produced more than 400,000 addicts during the war.

Doctors and patients came to rely on the instant relief supplied by morphine. In fact, it was used so often that the 1897 edition of the Sears Roebuck catalog offered a hypodermic kit—a syringe, two needles, two vials, and a handy carrying case for one's personal supply of morphine. The entire kit cost $1.50.

Not only were morphine and opium common medicines during these years in America's history, but many people also smoked opium recreationally. The practice was brought to America by the Chinese laborers who built the railroads across the country, and by 1875 opium smoking was particularly common among gamblers, prostitutes, and others who inhabited America's seamy underworld. However, many respectable men and women smoked opium as well. According to a report issued by the U.S. Public Health Service, almost 800 tons of smoking opium were imported into the United States between 1859 and 1899. During these years, as many as 3 million Americans may have been addicted to opium in one form or another.

Opium wasn't the only drug being legally used in America. In 1885, John Pemberton from Georgia developed a new product—French Wine Coca, Ideal Nerve and Tonic Stimulant. The concoction was derived from South American coca leaves (which contain the chemical found in cocaine) and cola nuts; it sold for a nickel per eight-ounce bottle, and it contained a good 60 milligrams of cocaine. However, since Pemberton's name for his new beverage was a bit

of a mouthful, the following year he shortened it to something more catchy—Coca-Cola.

In the 19th century, Coca Cola was a popular new beverage. In those days, every bottle contained 60 milligrams of cocaine.

Back in those days, Coke certainly was the "real thing." Pemberton described it this way:

> This "Intellectual Beverage" and Temperance Drink . . . makes not only a delicious, exhilarating, refreshing and invigorating Beverage . . . but a valuable Brain Tonic, and a cure for all nervous affections—Sick Head-ache, Neuralgia, Hysteria, Melancholy, &c.
>
> The peculiar flavor of COCA-COLA delights every palate; it is dispensed from the soda fountain in same manner as any of the fruit syrups.

Cocaine did indeed make its users feel good—at least temporarily—and like opium, it soon came to be used for a variety of ailments. Even Abraham Lincoln, shortly before the 1860 presidential election, purchased a bottle of cocaine for 50 cents at a drugstore; among

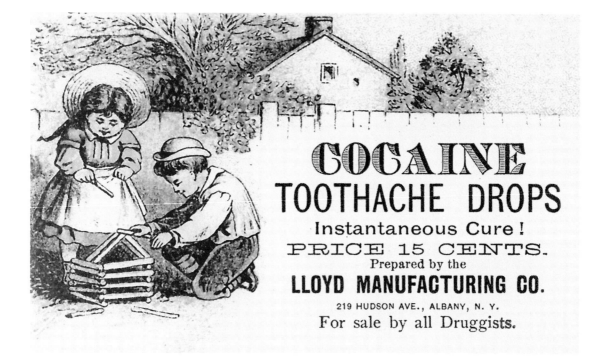

COCAINE
TOOTHACHE DROPS

Instantaneous Cure!
PRICE 15 CENTS.
Prepared by the
LLOYD MANUFACTURING CO.
219 HUDSON AVE., ALBANY, N. Y.
For sale by all Druggists.

This late-19th-century advertisement for a toothache medication indicates that cocaine was the crucial ingredient.

its many other supposed benefits, cocaine was thought to help grow beards.

Meanwhile, scientists were researching these amazing new medications, and late in the 19th century, codeine was invented. This drug is still available—by prescription—as a remedy for coughs. Another chemical compound called diacetylmorphine was also developed from opium. The new drug was said to be highly effective in treating coughs, chest pains, and the discomforts that went along with pneumonia and tuberculosis. Since these two diseases were among the leading causes of death—and antibiotics had still not been developed—doctors were excited. Bayer and Company (the same pharmaceutical company that would introduce aspirin a year later) began marketing this new wonder drug. Inspired by a German word meaning "heroic and powerful," Bayer called its new product Heroin.

Heroin was thought to be nonaddicting, and many

doctors turned to it as a "safe" alternative to morphine. Bayer advertised it as "the sedative for coughs." It was soon used in many other over-the-counter medications.

But by the early 20th century, medical science had progressed enough that doctors had a better understanding of drugs' long-term effects. The likelihood of addiction from opium- and cocaine-based drugs was now well known. The same doctors who had once advocated heroin (the capital *H* was dropped after the trade name found its way into everyday usage) and other medications now understood just how dangerous they could be.

Unfortunately, although doctors no longer recommended these drugs, people could still easily buy them. The medicine industry was unregulated by any laws, and many drugs were dangerously strong. Salespeople in colorfully decorated wagons brought many medicines to American towns. Medical journals warned of the dangers of these products—but no one but doctors read medical journals. Meanwhile, newspapers continued to advertise drugs that promised to cure Americans' every ill.

In 1905 the tide began to turn. *Colliers* magazine published a series of articles that year speaking out against what the magazine called the "Great American Fraud." The author of the series, Samuel Hopkins Adams, said in his opening essay:

> Gullible America will spend this year $75 million in the purchase of patent medicines. In consideration of this sum it will swallow huge quantities of alcohol, an appalling amount of opiates and narcotics, and [a] wide assortment of varied drugs ranging from powerful and dangerous . . . to insidious. . . . For fraud, exploited by the skillfullest of advertising men, is the basis of the trade.

Adams went on to say that this drug trade "stupefies helpless babies and makes criminals of our young men and harlots of our young women."

At about the same time that Adams was writing,

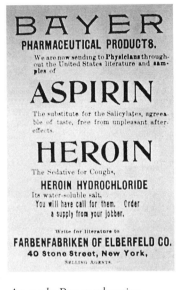

An early Bayer advertisement features two of the pharmaceutical company's new products: aspirin and heroin—a sedative for coughs.

Americans were also shocked by the work of another author, Upton Sinclair. Sinclair, however, did not write about drugs. In his book *The Jungle*, he described the terrible conditions within meat-packaging plants. Americans were horrified to learn that their sausage and other processed meats contained goat meat, dead rats, and even an occasional employee who slipped and fell into the vats.

The public's reaction to *The Jungle* led to the passage of the Pure Food and Drug Act in 1906. This act prohibited the interstate transportation of food or drugs that had been falsely labeled. This meant that all ingredients in medicines had to be revealed to consumers—and as a result, a number of "miraculous" medicines lost their appeal in the public's eye. Not wanting to lose sales, the makers of products like Coca-Cola decided to remove cocaine and other narcotics from their formulas. (These producers often used caffeine—another stimulant—instead.) The Pure Food and Drug Act, however, did not outlaw the use of cocaine- and opium-based drugs; it merely set standards for packaging and labeling, relying on public opinion to do the rest.

The first U.S. federal law to actually control the sale of drugs was the Harrison Act, which was put into effect in 1914. It required all people who imported, manufactured, produced, sold, or distributed in any way cocaine- and opium-based drugs to register with the Treasury Department. They also had to pay special taxes and keep records of all transactions.

Because of pressure from the pharmaceutical and tobacco companies, the law did not cover marijuana, tobacco, alcohol, nicotine, and caffeine. Furthermore, many legislators themselves smoked and kept snuffboxes of tobacco or marijuana on their desks; these men were unlikely to vote against products they enjoyed using.

The Harrison Act had other problems as well. Some historians feel that it pushed addicts out of society and

In 1911 President Theodore Roosevelt organized an international conference in China to discuss ways to control opium trafficking.

forced them into the crime world. The law was intended to give the government some control over drug producers, without punishing drug users, but since doctors could no longer legally prescribe drugs to addicts, addicts were forced to turn to black markets and crime. These people went from being patients to being criminals.

Other historians, though, note that as drug use was no longer socially acceptable, fewer and fewer respectable people used drugs. People who used drugs now were not members of the decent middle class; instead, they were criminals and other underworld characters. In any case, the use of drugs, particularly heroin, continued to increase at an alarming rate.

In 1911, President Theodore Roosevelt—worried

by the spread of the international opium trade and the organized crime that went with it from China to other parts of the world—organized a meeting of 13 nations in Shanghai. The first International Conference on Opium sought to control narcotics trafficking. The Hague Convention ratified the international regulation of opium in 1913 and 1914.

Meanwhile, Americans at home were more concerned with alcohol than they were with other addictive drugs. The temperance movement, backed by women's groups and church organizations, campaigned against alcohol, working to make it illegal. The women's rights movement was also under way, and many women spoke out loudly against "demon rum," focusing on the way alcohol hurt women's lives—for example, when drunken husbands beat them and their children or spent the family money on whiskey instead of food. In October 1919, the 18th Amendment to the Constitution, prohibiting the use of liquor throughout the United States, was passed.

In 1920, during the early stages of Prohibition, the League of Nations took responsibility for supervising agreements that pertained to opium and other dangerous drugs. At the same time, however, as many as 5 million Americans used heroin and cocaine. America was in the midst of a drug epidemic.

As a result, Americans began to call for more drug laws. The Jones-Miller Act set fines of up to $5,000 and imprisonment of up to 10 years for anyone involved with illegal drug trafficking. Unfortunately, the Jones-Miller Act had little effect—except to push up the price of drugs.

Prohibition was also doing little to control the use of alcohol throughout America. Speakeasies—or secret bars—were popular across the country, and organized crime supplied Americans with alcohol. Even government officials continued to drink in secret; President Warren Harding himself was known to drink whiskey

and beer privately in the White House. Worse, corruption flourished at all levels of government. For example, between 1920 and 1928, the Treasury Department fired 706 federal agents and prosecuted another 257 for taking bribes related to the sale of alcohol.

While Americans became disenchanted with Prohibition, they were also forced to admit that the use of narcotics was a serious problem in the United States. During the Roaring Twenties, cocaine plagued Hollywood to the point that movie mogul Louis B. Mayer complained, "If this keeps up, there won't be any motion picture industry." In response to people's outrage over

Prohibition agents confiscate a shipment of alcohol. Despite such interdiction efforts, the 18th Amendment ultimately failed to put an end to the sale and use of alcohol within the United States.

the portrayal of drug users in movies, 37 states passed censorship bills.

By now many people had realized that the drug problem existed—but they could not agree on how to handle the problem. Throughout the 1920s and 1930s, three different groups held three points of view: doctors argued that addiction should be treated as a physical disease; law-enforcement officials saw addiction as a crime and favored harsh punishment, believing stiff penalties would also help deter others from becoming drug users; and lawmakers believed they could make drug use nonexistent simply by passing enough laws making it illegal.

Doctors, law enforcers, and legislators each worked for their own set of goals. As a result, treatment facilities were opened, addicts were arrested and put in jail, and new laws were passed.

Although these three groups focused primarily on heroin and cocaine, in the 1930s more and more Americans became concerned about another drug: cannabis or hashish—what later came to be called marijuana.

Marijuana was used mostly by Mexican immigrants and blacks; Anglo-Americans feared it would "corrupt" white society. Lurid rumors spread that marijuana use was driving Mexicans insane, and as a result, state after state passed anti-marijuana laws. Concerned citizens, led by Harry J. Anslinger, the commissioner of the Treasury Department's Bureau of Narcotics, pressured Washington for federal legislation against the drug. Eventually, on August 2, 1937, the Marijuana Tax Act was signed. This law classified the marijuana plant as a narcotic and placed it under the same controls as those imposed on opium and cocaine products by the Harrison Act.

While marijuana use grew during World War II, heroin and cocaine use decreased, since the war cut off the supply routes from Asia through Europe. However, within three years after the war's end, illegal narcotics

once again began to reach American ports. With the drugs came crime.

As Americans moved into the second half of the 20th century, they were forced to recognize that drugs were a very real threat to the nation's safety. But while people agreed on the problem, they were less sure about the solution. In the years to come, the American government would struggle to find the answer, and the American people would be divided in their attitude toward drug legislation. Some wanted tougher drug laws—and some wanted drugs to be legalized again.

Marijuana was legal until passage of the Marijuana Tax Act in 1937. Many white Americans had become fearful that marijuana, widely believed to be the drug of choice among Mexican immigrants and blacks, would destroy American society.

3

CHANGING VIEWPOINTS

The second half of the 20th century brought many new ideas about drugs. Like a pendulum swinging back and forth, over the last 50 years, Americans have changed their minds again and again about the dangers of drugs. Overall, however, while the public may have gone back and forth on the drug issue, the government has tended to pass tougher and tougher drug laws. Today, the manufacture, sale, and use of illegal drugs are all serious crimes.

But back in the 1950s, many people in the United States considered drugs to be merely a ghetto problem. Racism was strong among middle-class white Americans, who were unwilling to face the fact that drugs were a problem that belonged to everyone.

As the 1950s gave way to the 1960s, however, America witnessed a drug revolution. Suddenly, drug use was no longer confined to the inner cities and the bohemian world of jazz musicians and movie stars; now drugs leapt to the mainstream of American

In the 1960s, Americans' views on drugs underwent a change. Increasing numbers of young people experimented not only with marijuana and opium derivatives such as heroin but also with powerful hallucinogens such as LSD.

communities. Everywhere across both rural and urban America, middle-class adolescents and young adults were using drugs.

During the decade of the '60s, the Vietnam War and the sexual revolution became linked with the use of "grass," one of the many slang terms for marijuana. Liberal attitudes toward peace and freedom led to experiments with mind-altering substances. One college professor even made this prediction: "psychedelic drugs will be used in all schools in the near future as educational devices . . . to teach kids how to use their sense organs and cellular equipment more effectively." Obviously, this prophecy has not come true; today we work to keep drugs out of our schools.

However, at that time, smoking marijuana became an antiauthority symbol among young people who opposed the war in Southeast Asia, a war that was allegedly being waged by the adult "establishment." Meanwhile, in Vietnam, American soldiers were using "pot" (yet another slang term for marijuana); the military panicked over the breach in security and the danger to troops operating heavy equipment and arms while stoned, or intoxicated. When the Army cracked down on pot, some soldiers switched to heroin, which was odorless, less bulky, and inexpensive in Vietnam. Unfortunately, it was also extremely addictive.

Back home, drug use was no longer considered secret and shady. Instead, singers like Bob Dylan captivated the youth culture with song lyrics that claimed "everybody must get stoned." The Beatles sang of "Lucy in the Sky with Diamonds"; Lucy's initials, of course, were LSD. And in 1969 in Woodstock, New York, a star-studded rock concert was attended by 400,000 young people—and drugs were everywhere.

LSD—the chemical compound lysergic acid diethylamide—was the new drug on the scene in the '60s. It had been developed in 1938 by Dr. Albert Hoffman, a scientist in Switzerland who had no idea

Smoking marijuana became a symbol of young peoples' rebellion against authority in the '60s.

what he had stumbled across. Five years later, though, Hoffman accidentally absorbed some of the compound through the skin of his fingers. He began to hallucinate, "seeing" sounds as a kaleidoscope of color. Hoffman had experienced the first LSD "trip."

Scientists referred to the new drug as "psychedelic," meaning that it was mind-expanding, but at the beginning of the 1960s virtually no one outside the scientific community had even heard of LSD. That quickly changed when Professor Timothy Leary of Harvard University began to experiment on himself with LSD. Soon after, he formed the International Foundation for Internal Freedom, which promoted the use of psychedelics as a basic human right. Like a modern-day Pied Piper, Leary told young Americans: "*Turn on* to the scene, *tune in* to what's happening; and *drop out*—of

Professor Timothy Leary of Harvard University not only experimented with LSD himself, but also encouraged young people to use the drug as well.

high school, college, grade school . . . follow me. . . ."

Parents and other adults were horrified by Leary's message, and toward the end of the 1960s and early 1970s, the mood of the country began to change. People were frightened by the LSD drug scene because, in their minds, LSD was connected with long-haired, unwashed "hippies" who intentionally rejected a rational system of law and order. Further, reports of "bad trips" and flashbacks caused rumors that LSD could literally "blow your mind."

For these reasons, LSD was not widely used on a regular basis throughout the country. LSD and other psychedelic drugs quickly earned the reputation of being dangerous, and by the end of the 1960s they had been placed under strict legal regulations.

The 1960s' "flower children" had believed drugs were innocent substances that would help them grasp the meaning of life more easily, but these beliefs were shattered by an increasing number of drug tragedies. In 1970 rock stars Jimi Hendrix and Janis Joplin both died of drug overdoses, and the daughter of television host Art Linkletter killed herself during a bad LSD trip.

In response, the government's authority to determine which drugs were illegal was transferred from the surgeon general to the attorney general; this meant that drugs were now seen as a crime issue rather than a health threat. As people became more and more aware of the drug problem, Congress sent millions of dollars to clinics where heroin addicts were treated.

While public attention may have focused on heroin and LSD, law enforcers were aware that the United States had another drug problem as well: during the 1960s the number of people who had tried marijuana at least once shot up from a few hundred thousand to about 8 million. In 1969, in response to these numbers, the federal government decided that the best way to curb marijuana use would be to keep marijuana from entering the country from Mexico. "Operation Intercept" was launched, tightening the inspection of vehicles coming into the United States across the Mexican border in an attempt to keep smuggled drugs out of America.

As a result of Operation Intercept, the lines at the border stretched out as far as six miles. Mexico complained to the U.S. Congress that tourism was being hurt; American travelers complained because of the extra hours spent waiting to cross the border; and merchants complained because their businesses were being hurt. After only 20 days, the American government brought the operation to an end.

Operation Intercept did accomplish two things: more marijuana began to be imported from Vietnam, and more Americans began to grow their own marijuana. The drug's popularity continued to grow. In fact, many otherwise law-abiding people smoked pot. As a result, the federal government introduced legislation that reduced the penalties for possession of marijuana. Many states followed the federal government's example.

Meanwhile, heroin continued to be the drug American society feared the most, with LSD running a close second. But all the while public attention was focused on heroin and LSD and even marijuana, two other groups of drugs that most Americans ignored—amphetamines and barbiturates—were creeping into the country.

These drugs were not new—they had first been created in the 1880s in Germany—but they were not used on the street until after World War II. During the war, thousands of servicemen used amphetamines to fight their anxiety and exhaustion, and after the war, the drug began to be used by many people for many reasons, from women wanting to lose weight to students cramming for exams. By the end of the 1960s, enough amphetamines were being produced to dose every American 50 times per year, while the annual production of barbiturates—drugs that have a sedative, or tranquilizing, effect—was equal to 24 one-and-one-half-grain doses for every U.S. resident. Most of these drugs were legal at the time.

In the '70s, President Richard Nixon launched the "War on Drugs" as part of a larger crackdown on crime and violence. One of the first groups of drugs the government tackled was amphetamines. Tighter controls were placed on prescribing and distributing these drugs, and the legal manufacture of amphetamines was reduced by 90 percent.

By 1974 the federal drug budget had leapt to $719 million, compared with only $69 million in 1969. But despite all the money spent, Nixon's War on Drugs was not totally successful. By the mid-1970s, a political scandal known as Watergate had engulfed Nixon's presidency (he resigned in 1974) and derailed his policies, including his antidrug campaign. After Nixon's resignation, drug policy analysts working for President Gerald Ford concluded that eliminating drug abuse entirely was an unrealistic goal. For instance, researchers found that young people who had been using amphetamines had simply turned to another drug —methaqualone, or Quaalude—when amphetamines became less available.

Methaqualone was first produced in India in the 1950s as a medicine for treating malaria. Later, the drug was also found to help people sleep, and many doctors turned to it as an alternative to barbiturates, which were known to be both habit-forming and potentially lethal. In the 1960s, William H. Rorer, the same pharmaceutical company that manufactured the antacid Maalox, introduced methaqualone to Americans; the double-a had proved catchy in the antacid's name, and so Rorer called its new drug Quaalude. The manufacturer emphasized that it was a safe substitute for barbiturates, and free samples were shipped across the country.

Quaalude could not be purchased in the United States without a prescription, but federal drug controllers thought that since Quaalude could not be abused, it did not need to be monitored as carefully; prescriptions for it could be refilled an unlimited number of times. Almost immediately, American doctors began over-prescribing the drug.

As things turned out, Quaalude was not a safe alternative to anything. It was just as addictive and just as dangerous as the drugs it had replaced. After amphetamines were no longer readily available on the street because of tighter drug laws, reports soon began to spread that Quaalude was being abused to the same degree that amphetamines had been. Users often had extreme—and sometimes fatal—reactions to the new drug.

At a series of Senate hearings, methaqualone's problems were thoroughly revealed, and rigid laws were put into effect to control its sale in any form. Shortly thereafter, Quaalude abuse began to decline. Eventually, laws were passed that put an end to all legal manufacture of methaqualone in the United States.

HOW DANGEROUS IS MARIJUANA?
COMPARED TO OTHER SUBSTANCES?

NUMBER OF AMERICAN DEATHS PER YEAR

TOBACCO	340,000 to 450,000
ALCOHOL	150,000
ASPIRIN	180 to 1,000
CAFFEINE	1000 to 10,000
LEGAL DRUG OVERDOSE	14,000 to 27,000
ILLICIT DRUG OVERDOSE	3800 to 5,200
MARIJUANA	0

The owner of this truck makes the case for legalizing marijuana. The debate over whether that would be a good idea has raged since the 1970s.

And all the while, throughout the '70s, the country seesawed between extreme reactions for and against drugs. Some people wanted to make drugs legal again, and in 1970 the National Organization for the Reform of Marijuana Laws (NORML) was founded. Three years later, however, the New York State legislature went to the other extreme and passed the Rockefeller Drug Laws, calling for up to 15 years behind bars for possession of a mere ounce of marijuana and life in prison for an ounce of heroin.

Reflecting this same strong stance against drugs, Congress created the Drug Enforcement Administration as part of the Justice Department to help put an end to illegal drug trafficking. In 1978, the DEA gained the power to confiscate money and property belonging to suspected drug dealers, and in 1980 the DEA developed model drug laws, which were circulated among state legislatures, banning drug-related paraphernalia like papers for rolling marijuana joints (cigarettes), water pipes, seeds for hemp plants (a close cousin to the cannabis—or marijuana—plant), needles, and syringes.

And yet as the country entered a new decade, drug use persisted. In 1981 President Ronald Reagan ordered the Federal Bureau of Investigation to go after drug dealers. The FBI's drug budget went up 50 percent, and the Coast Guard's drug budget rose 44 percent. Despite their efforts, however, throughout the 1980s, crack (crystallized or "rock" cocaine) wreaked havoc on America's inner cities.

This new form of cocaine was both extremely addictive and extremely dangerous. According to historian Dr. Jill Jonnes, crack cocaine made heroin "look like the good old days." In her book *Hep Cats, Narcs, and Pipe-Dreams: A History of America's Romance with Illegal Drugs*, Jonnes notes that while crack might have been new to the American drug scene, scientists were aware of cocaine's devastating impact 100 years earlier. As early as 1885, one New York doctor warned in a medical journal that cocaine is "the most powerful and devilish drug which it has ever been the misfortune of man to abuse." This 19th-century doctor's words proved terribly true in the 1980s as "crack houses" (where cocaine was sold and used) and "crack babies" (infants damaged by cocaine before they were ever born) marked a new and terrible stage in the history of drug abuse.

In 1986—the same year the military reported cutting drug use by half—Boston Celtics draft pick Len Bias and football's Don Rogers of the Cleveland Browns both died from cocaine, proving that just one dose could be lethal even to healthy young athletes. That same year President Reagan signed an executive

In 1978 Congress created the Drug Enforcement Administration, and in 1980, as part of a broad campaign, the DEA developed model laws that banned drug-related paraphernalia such as this paper for rolling marijuana joints.

order for a "Drug-Free Workplace," requiring federal agencies to check employees' urine for traces of illegal drugs. Workers who tested positive might receive treatment and counseling—or they might be fired.

Meanwhile, crack had a deadly influence on neighborhoods and communities. It spawned violence among rival drug gangs fighting turf battles, while crack addicts were driven to crime in order to sustain their habits. In response, federal laws were passed that gave the death penalty to drug lords. The government also repealed the exclusionary rule that barred illegally obtained evidence from admission in drug trials. Criminals convicted of violating drug laws could not receive suspended sentences or probation. As more and more people were sent to prison, a billion dollars was set aside for building new prisons.

However, government officials began to realize they could not rely only on harsh drug laws to control the drug problem. In 1992, President Bush started the federal "Weed and Seed" program to *weed* out drug dealers— particularly in minority communities—and *seed* neighborhoods with social services and educational opportunities. Bill Clinton became president the same year, and his new surgeon general, Joycelyn Elders, told the National Press Club that crime might decrease if drugs were legalized. In the face of considerable criticism over this issue and others, Clinton fired Elders. Next, retired general Barry McCaffrey, Clinton's director of the Office of National Drug Control Policy, attracted the support of both Democrats and Republicans. Favoring a combination of demand and supply reduction, McCaffrey's number-one concern was teaching young people to reject illegal drugs, including cigarettes and alcohol. With $195 million budgeted by Congress, McCaffrey launched an antidrug campaign targeting youngsters with paid advertisements in magazines and on television, radio, the Internet, and other

electronic media. McCaffrey also favored treatment for nonviolent offenders so that the enormous number of imprisoned Americans could be reduced.

In the past, as laws were enacted that made some drugs less available, use of those drugs often declined—but at the same time, criminal involvement in the manufacture and sale of the drugs increased. The tighter laws also drove up the drugs' prices, and this in turn attracted criminals who were eager to make their fortune trafficking, manufacturing, and dealing illegal drugs.

Today, the government is looking at other options for decreasing drug use, options that extend beyond the criminal justice system. Ultimately, these new solutions may help resolve America's drug dilemma. In the meantime, however, drugs and crime continue to go hand in hand.

President Bill Clinton looks on as Barry McCaffrey, Director of the Office of National Drug Control Policy, speaks at a 1999 press conference. During the 1990s, McCaffrey launched a campaign to help young people reject illegal drugs.

THE DRUG-CRIME CONNECTION

4

Recently, a local newspaper reported that a teenage boy was caught shoplifting radios in order to get money to buy drugs. The next month, the same newspaper reported that a 15-year-old girl turned to prostitution to support her drug habit, and a husband beat up his wife because she helped herself to his stash of drugs without telling him. The same month, according to the newspaper, two friends came to blows because one refused to share his drug supply with the other. The following week, a woman stabbed her boyfriend because he didn't buy enough drugs to share with her. Only a few months later, another drug dealer murdered one of his sellers when the dealer discovered that the seller had been dipping into the drugs without paying.

Another newspaper told the story of a woman who was raped by a drug dealer when she bought drugs from him. The next week, when she went

Because they constantly need more money to support their habit, drug users are responsible for many property crimes, such as burglary.

45

back for more, she was raped again.

Yet another news story described an incident involving a wealthy businessman who was mugged while walking the streets of New York City. When his attacker found that the businessman was carrying only a $10 bill, the attacker became furious because he had hoped for enough money to supply his need for heroin. In a rage, the attacker beat the businessman unconscious.

And last but certainly not least, a Florida newspaper told of an angry drug lord who decided to get rid of the competition. His hit van pulled up to a store owned by Colombian drug traffickers, and machine-gun fire sprayed everyone in sight. The Colombians were killed and several bystanders were wounded.

These actual events all tell the same story: drugs lead to crime. One reason for this is that drugs cost money, while they rob users of the ability to hold down a job. As a user's addiction increases, he becomes less and less able to concentrate or perform intellectual or physical tasks, and he may be fired. Or, as a user's life becomes more and more focused on drugs, she is apt to drop out of the workforce.

Even if a drug user manages to hold down a job, drugs—heroin in particular—are too expensive for most users to buy out of their paychecks. Meanwhile, the need for drugs can be desperate and overwhelming. Users may be unwilling or unable to accommodate their drug habits to the demands of a job; criminal activities, however, allow them to get money as fast as possible, rather than having to wait for payday. Crime allows users the flexibility to set their schedules to coincide with the demands of their habit.

In Ari Kiev's book *The Drug Epidemic*, he interviewed a young addict named Danny. Danny described the way he supported his habit:

I have committed more than five hundred, six hundred crimes. . . . I would try anything. I went from snatching pocketbooks to beating old ladies [to get their money] to everything I could think of to get money for drugs.

I was stealing welfare checks too. . . . I also stole checks from this job I used to work. . . . The only feeling that I had was to get money to support my habit. After I got the money and got high I'd think, oh, I shouldn't have done this and it wasn't right. But a dope fiend don't care.

For many drug users, violent crime becomes a way of life.

Danny's words indicate another aspect of the crime-drug connection: drugs break down inhibitions. Danny may have once been a moral person, but now he can barely hear the voice of his conscience; his habit's demands are far louder. What's more, drug users like Danny know they are already breaking the law simply by using illegal drugs; breaking yet another law by committing a robbery does not seem that important to them. Lawbreaking becomes a way of life.

Drugs may also lead to crime because the drug itself makes the user crave excitement. According to another of the young addicts interviewed in Kiev's book, "there's nothing more thrilling, nothing more exciting, than to be speeding [using cocaine mixed with heroin] and have the excitement of knowing you're going to break into a store. That was the greatest feeling I ever had." Users like this may drive too fast or take other physical risks—but more times than not they find their excitement in crime.

In the 19th century, few Americans connected drug use with crime. But by the 1970s this connection was firmly fixed in the American mind. A 1972 Gallup poll found that almost half of those surveyed were afraid to walk in their neighborhoods at night, and drug addiction was given as the major reason for the high crime rate. By 1973, Gallup rated crime as the nation's greatest urban problem, with drug use ranking third.

President Nixon responded to these findings by saying, "We have regarded drugs as 'public enemy number one,' destroying the most precious resource we have—our young people—and breeding lawlessness, violence, and death."

Nixon's administration had indeed spent millions of dollars on his so-called War on Drugs, but his critics wondered if he was exaggerating the close connection between crime and drugs. In 1975, the National Institute on Drug Abuse (NIDA) convened a meeting to establish a federal plan for researching the drug-crime connection. The National Institute of Justice also funded a series of studies.

The studies done by these two organizations found a number of things to be true. First, heroin users engaged in a far greater number of crimes when they were addicted than when they were in treatment. Second, the studies found that during a one-year period, active addicts experienced an average of 230 "crime-days" (24-hour periods during which an individual committed at least one crime). And last, these researchers found that the number of crimes committed by drug users was far greater than anyone had ever suspected, and these crimes were often extremely violent. The studies also concluded that the violence was so great that it was beyond the control of law enforcement.

Specifically, these research studies found that:

- 99.5 percent of all heroin users had committed a criminal offense.
- The first crime committed by 25 percent of all narcotics users was shoplifting.
- 13 percent of all female drug users began their criminal activity with prostitution.
- 21 percent of all narcotics users had assaulted someone.
- 53 percent were burglars.
- 38 percent were forgers.
- 22 percent were prostitutes.
- 84 percent were drug sellers.
- Almost all narcotics users were thieves.

Not surprisingly, people who did not use narcotic drugs had much lower rates of committing these crimes. Perhaps the most disturbing finding, however, was that only 1 percent of the crimes ever led to arrest. In other words, most drug users were getting away with their crimes.

Researchers in the drug field conclude that heroin addicts are responsible for as many as 50 million crimes each year in the United States. An equal number may be committed by users of cocaine and other drugs. Drugs have created an American nightmare.

In response to this research, police and other law enforcers have intensified their struggle to control drug-related crime. The legal response to drug crimes varies from state to state, and police procedures may differ from community to community. However, one thing is true across America: if you're arrested for the possession of an illegal drug, you will face legal consequences.

5.

DRUG POLICY AND CRIMINAL JUSTICE

One summer night Jimmy Townsley was hanging out in the park with his friends. They shot some hoops for a while, and then they sat on the ground and relaxed, sharing the drugs they had with them. Jimmy was feeling sleepy and contented when suddenly the cops burst into the park. The informal party had been busted.

Jimmy was locked up for the night. His cell had no mattresses on the beds, and his cellmate was an adult man who was stone drunk. The man smelled bad, and he grunted and shouted in his sleep, scaring Jimmy so badly he could scarcely breathe. Jimmy had heard lots of stories about jail and the terrible things that went on there. He stayed awake all night, shivering on the bare bed. He wasn't sure what to expect next.

What actually happened after Jimmy was arrested would depend on several factors. For instance, most states have mandatory sentences (punishments that are already spelled out by law) for the possession of certain

51

Individuals arrested for the possession of an illegal drug will likely spend at least some time in a jail or prison cell.

illegal substances, while only a few states would leave the sentence up to the judge's discretion. Mandatory sentences vary from state to state, so Jimmy's sentence would depend partly on where he lived. If he escaped a mandatory sentence, then the consequences of Jimmy's drug use would depend on the strictness of the individual judge who heard his case. His sentence would also depend on other factors, such as his age, what kind of drug he was using, and whether he had a previous record.

If Jimmy were over 16, most states would try him as an adult, and he would likely face criminal penalties for his little party in the park. For a first offense of simple possession (where only a small amount of drugs are involved and there is no evidence that drugs were being sold), an offender would probably receive a fine or probation. If, however, the offender already has a record of previous drug use, the judge might hand down a sentence of time in jail or prison. Many court systems, though, will give an addicted offender treatment rather than imprisonment.

In general, America's antidrug efforts take a two-pronged approach: first, reducing the demand for drugs through treatment programs and education; and second, reducing the supply of drugs through law enforcement. Many critics have suggested that demand-reduction efforts—in particular, treatment programs—are woefully underfunded. But the illegal drug problem is enormous and complicated, and solutions are elusive.

Over the past 20 years, drug policies have had an enormous impact on the entire criminal justice system. In the 1980s, President Reagan launched his own "War on Drugs," increasing funding for drug law enforcement. The U.S. Congress and state legislators passed strict antidrug laws. As a result, the number of arrests for drug offenses nearly tripled. (In 1980, there were 581,000 arrests for drug offenses; in 1997 there were 1,584,000.) American courts and prisons today are crowded with drug offenders.

Meanwhile, critics of the War on Drugs point to a disturbing fact: although the number of people using drugs has decreased dramatically over the past 20 years, the number of arrests continues to remain at record highs. These critics are also bothered by the harsher sentences that are now handed down to drug offenders, including mandatory prison time. These mandatory sentences have filled American prisons with drug offenders, taking space away from offenders who may have committed more serious and violent crimes.

As a result of mandatory sentencing laws, between 1980 and 1992 the chances of receiving a prison term after being arrested for a drug offense rose by 447 percent.

Mandatory sentencing laws first became popular with Americans in the 1980s as crime rates soared and people became more and more afraid of drug-related violence. In particular, both politicians and the public supported mandatory sentencing for large-scale drug dealers; Americans wanted to make sure the law guaranteed that those who were guilty of these serious crimes would spend time in prison. By 1983, 49 states had adopted some form of mandatory sentencing.

Today, every state and the federal court system have some type of mandatory sentencing laws that require imprisonment. If drug offenders are tried in federal rather than state court, they come under the mandatory minimum penalties that Congress adopted in 1986 and 1988. These mandatory sentencing laws are among the strictest in the country, and until recently they required a mandatory five-year prison term for possessing as little as five grams of crack cocaine.

It may seem logical that mandatory sentencing would guarantee harsher punishment for people caught violating drug laws. But studies have shown that this is not necessarily the case. In fact, in some states where mandatory sentencing laws are in effect, fewer offenders, not more, have actually gone to prison.

This unexpected result can be explained, at least in part, by the discretion criminal justice officials have and by the opinion of these officials that in individual cases the prescribed sentence would be unduly harsh. Prosecutors, for example, might decide to charge a drug offender with a crime that isn't covered by a mandatory minimum sentence. Judges also may reduce the charges against a defendant. In addition, deals are often made, so that defendants escape conviction as a reward for turning in other criminals.

For people actually convicted under mandatory sentencing laws, the likelihood of imprisonment and the average length of prison terms are both increased— but these patterns are canceled out by the fact that

conviction rates decrease when mandatory sentencing laws are in effect. The overall chance of being imprisoned ends up being about the same after the mandatory sentencing laws were passed as it was before.

Most Americans believed that severe mandatory sentences would decrease drug crime. After all, if potential drug dealers *knew* they would receive stiff punishment if caught, wouldn't many be deterred from breaking the law in the first place? And wouldn't the laws eventually take a great many of those not deterred off the streets?

Despite these commonsense assumptions, the Rand Drug Policy Research Center found that even when mandatory sentences are handed down, they

President Ronald Reagan increased funding for drug law enforcement. In the 1980s, his administration favored the tough War on Drugs stance taken by the Nixon administration a decade earlier.

Drug laws have contributed greatly to America's high incarceration rate, particularly among minorities.

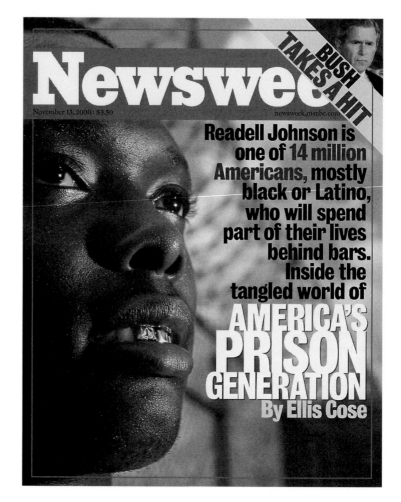

Newsweek

November 13, 2000 : $3.50   newsweek.msnbc.com

BUSH TAKES A HIT

Readell Johnson is one of 14 million Americans, mostly black or Latino, who will spend part of their lives behind bars. Inside the tangled world of AMERICA'S PRISON GENERATION
By Ellis Cose

are ineffective at controlling the level of drug crime in America. Because the demand for illegal drugs remains high, and profits from the drug trade are enormous, there is no shortage of people willing to assume the risks of dealing drugs. So when a drug dealer is imprisoned, he or she is simply replaced by another dealer. The Rand research concluded that the money spent through the justice system on mandatory sentences might be put to better use if it were spent instead on drug treatment programs.

Mandatory sentencing has other flaws as well. For instance, under certain statutes, any member of a drug gang is punishable for the total amount of drugs sold by the entire organization. Thus a low-level courier or dealer might receive the same sentence as the gang's so-called kingpin. But the low-level courier or dealer is much more likely to be caught than the kingpin. And, when they are caught, senior members of a drug gang have something to trade for more lenient treatment—the names of other members of the organization. Street dealers, on the other hand, typically have little to offer prosecutors in order to make a deal.

Research conducted by the U.S. Sentencing Commission in 1992 found that 55 percent of federal drug defendants were low-level street dealers, 34 percent were mid-level dealers, and only 11 percent were high-level dealers. And yet putting drug kingpins away for long prison terms would better serve the goals of reducing the flow of drugs and increasing public safety.

Mandatory sentencing has many critics. Congress continues to reassess legislation that relates to drug crimes, and new bills have been passed to help make the legal system more fair. New approaches are also being tried to handle drug crimes.

One of these new approaches is special courts that offer drug treatment as an alternative to prison terms for nonviolent offenders who have substance abuse problems. Defendants who complete the drug-court program either have their charges dismissed or their sentences (or probation) reduced. Today, there are nearly 400 drug courts across the United States, up from the mere dozen that existed in 1994. According to S. Belenko in an article in *National Drug Court Institute Review*, nearly 100,000 people have been diverted from the regular courts to drug courts.

Drug courts seem to be more effective than other community treatment programs for several reasons.

First of all, they reach drug users who have never been in treatment before. When facing prison as an alternative, these people are often motivated to give up drugs entirely or at least greatly reduce their use. Drug-court programs also supervise their participants more closely than other treatment programs do; the drug-court programs require frequent blood and urine tests for drugs, status hearings, and face-to-face meetings with probation officers.

Drug use drops for graduates of these programs— and so does criminal behavior. Many counties that use drug courts have reported that they save money that would have otherwise been spent on the criminal justice system. For instance, Multnomah County in Oregon saved $2.5 million over 2 years; Honolulu saved between $677,000 and $854,000 a year; and Riverside County in California saved $2 million a year.

Drug courts are usually designed for adult offenders, but by 2001 there were at least 35 juvenile drug courts in the United States. Early results indicate that their success rates match those of their adult counterparts. When young people were asked to identify the factors most likely to help them stay drug-free, they came up with the following list:

- Consistent monitoring and support from probation officers.
- Having to face a judge and explain their behavior.
- Urine testing.
- Positive reinforcement from drug treatment teams.
- High expectations from the court.
- Not wanting to disappoint themselves or the treatment staff.

All of these factors are provided by the drug-court treatment programs.

Drug courts seem to be an effective new approach to drug crimes. Unfortunately, this approach reaches only 3 percent of drug offenders who go through the U.S. criminal justice system.

The judicial system alone cannot handle the American drug problem; that approach would be a bit like trying to close the barn door after the horse has escaped, when a far wiser course of action would be to close the door *before* the horse runs away. That's why more and more the U.S. government endorses education as a way to *prevent* drug abuse. This approach combined with treatment of those who are already addicted may be the best way to reduce substance abuse in America.

In the meantime, however, the connection between drugs and crime continues to be very real. And if you get busted more than once for using or selling drugs, you're likely to end up in prison.

A woman hugs her nine-month-old child while she waits to appear before a drug court. The mother was arrested on a drug charge, but she claims she wants to go straight now and stay out of jail so she can care for her daughter. The drug court's treatment sentencing will give her that option.

REHAB BEHIND BARS?

The Attica Correctional Facility houses some of New York State's 70,000 prisoners. Because a substantial percentage of America's prisoners are drug offenders, observers argue that drug rehabilitation programs should be an integral part of prison life.

Between 1980 and 2000, the number of incarcerated Americans more than tripled. By 1999, more than 1.8 million people were serving sentences in American jails and prisons; many of them were drug users. According to statistics from the Sentencing Project—a Washington, D.C.–based organization that analyzes criminal justice policy—in 1980, 6 percent of all inmates in state prisons and 25 percent in federal prisons were drug offenders. By 1996, the proportion of drug offenders had climbed to 23 percent of all state prison inmates and 60 percent of all federal prison inmates. These numbers would go even higher if they included inmates who were sentenced for drug-related offenses (for instance, a burglary committed to get money for drugs or an assault committed by a person under the influence of drugs). More than half of state prison inmates in 1997 had used drugs in the month before their arrest, and about one-sixth of them committed their crime in order to obtain drug money.

Once these people complete their sentences, most quickly resume the drug habit that put them in prison in the first place.

Because so many drug addicts are serving time, America's prisons would be a good place to offer drug treatment. Studies have proved that even when people are *forced* to undergo therapy to help them kick their drug habits, their chances of successfully quitting increase. Unfortunately, only a small proportion of inmates have that option. Although other rehabilitation programs may be available within prisons, these can do little good if an inmate's addiction is not addressed. Consequently, the Clinton administration launched a national campaign to increase drug treatment programs in all prisons.

Of course, not all treatment programs are equally effective. Research shows that therapy needs to last longer than 90 days, and follow-up is essential. Sociology and criminal justice professor James Inciardi's Key-Crest program in Delaware demonstrated that prisoners who took part in a work-release program after their in-prison drug treatment were more than twice as likely to remain drug-free and a third more likely to be arrest-free 18 months after their release from prison, compared with inmates who did not receive this level of supervision and support. When drug treatment is combined with other forms of rehabilitation—like literacy and job training—it is also more likely to have lasting results.

Doctors like Alan Leshner of the National Institute of Drug Abuse claim that addicts are not simply "bad" people who deserve to be punished. Instead, these doctors look at addiction as a form of disease. They insist that because drugs change the chemistry of the brain, addicts need help and support before they can get off drugs. Jeremy Travis, director of the National Institute of Justice, agrees with this point of view; he argues that drug treatment should be a part of the U.S.

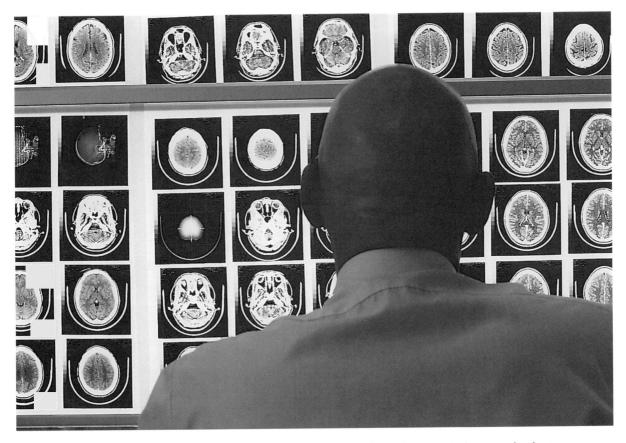

A doctor studies brain scan images. Drug addiction can change the chemistry and structure of the brain.

prison system as a form of "risk management." In other words, if prisons give convicts the treatment they need, then the system is not only helping the individual inmate; it is also helping to protect society from the future crimes that individual might otherwise commit.

"The ultimate goal of criminal justice," Travers asserts, "should be to strengthen, in the life of the offender, the naturally coercive powers of family, work, positive peer pressure, neighbors—what we call informal social controls." One way to build these powers is through intensive inmate drug treatment programs.

Some Americans feel that their tax dollars should not go to providing therapy for convicts, but in reality this is a very practical approach to drug abuse. Building and maintaining prisons is a heavy burden that may interfere with other societal goals. America now builds more new prisons than new schools, and the cost of the U.S. prison system has soared. The cost to taxpayers of keeping a person imprisoned is about $25,000 a year. According to a study conducted by the California Department of Alcohol and Drug Programs and the National Opinion Research Center, treatment programs reduce future criminal activity by as much as two-thirds—and they cost about 10 percent of the price of a prison cell. Because prisoners who receive treatment are far less likely to be imprisoned again, an investment in treatment programs makes good financial sense.

When we think in terms of society's safety, treatment programs continue to make sense. Joseph Califano Jr., chairperson of the National Center on Addiction and Substance Abuse at Columbia University, speculated that if the current numbers of prison sentences continue, 1 in 20 Americans born in 1997 will spend some of their lives in prison. The odds look worse for men, and worse still for African-American men. (One in every four black men will spend some time in prison.) Given these numbers, releasing addicted inmates without treating them, Califano observed, is like intentionally flooding society with criminals. In 1994, 31,000 inmates took part in federal drug treatment programs; a study of these inmates six months after their release, when most inmates would be back to using drugs, found that this group was 73 percent less likely to be arrested again for a drug-related crime. They were also 44 percent less likely to use drugs at all, compared with those prisoners who had received no treatment. This means that American society is safer as a result.

The Federal Bureau of Prisons now offers drug treatment to eligible prison inmates, and the number of prisons providing this treatment has risen from 32 to 42 since 1994. However, this encouraging trend is

undermined by other statistics. For example, the Sentencing Project reported that although more treatment programs were available, only 1 in 10 inmates were actually receiving treatment in 1997, compared with 1 in 4 in 1991.

Part of the problem may be the availability of illegal drugs within most prisons. In some of Florida's jails, for instance, an investigation found that in return for cash, jewelry, and sports equipment, police officers looked the other way when marijuana and cocaine were brought to inmates. Although this particular investigation involved only Dade County Jail and Turner Guilford

Early morning prayer and therapy are part of this drug rehabilitation facility's program. When prison inmates are able to participate in drug treatment programs like this one, they are less likely to go back to using drugs after their release.

Knight Correctional Center, similar allegations have been made about other jails and prisons.

In the same way, some prison guards are guilty of contributing to the problem of drugs within prisons. Some illegal drugs, however, are sent to prisoners through the mail or hidden in food packages delivered by friends or family. Sometimes, inmates on work-release bring drugs back with them when they return to jail.

State governments are combating the problem of drugs in prisons. Different institutions use various approaches. To prevent drug use and catch users, some prisons have inmates undergo urine or hair analysis to detect the presence of illegal drugs. Other institutions use dogs to search for drugs, or an electric version of canine searches that employs an expensive vacuum-cleaner-like machine that sucks up residue from skin, hair, or clothing, and then tests the results within seconds. The machine can detect even one-billionth of a gram of narcotics. These machines are already being used in Pennsylvania state prisons, and New Jersey prisons plan to make this technology a part of their "zero-tolerance policy" toward drugs.

The federal government is also looking for ways to control drug use within the prison system. The Office of National Drug Control Policy (ONDCP), the National Institute of Corrections, and the Federal Bureau of Prisons have jointly undertaken a $6 million plan to reduce illegal drug use in prisons. Another program, the Drug-Free Prison Zone Demonstration Project, began in federal prisons in 1998. This project's activities include regular inmate testing for drugs, advanced machines for detecting illegal drugs, and training for the prison staff. The ONDCP found that in two sample prisons in Tucson and Los Angeles, serious drug-related behaviors had gone down by 58 to 86 percent. In 1999, state prisons also began using this project to counteract prison drug use.

Despite these and other initiatives to combat drug abuse, major obstacles remain. In the December 2, 1998, issue of the *Boston Globe*, Thomas Delaney described the mindset of many of the young drug users he treated from 1993 to 1994 in a New York State abuse rehabilitation center. These young, mostly African-American men seemed to take it for granted that prison was a part of life; they spoke of going upstate to prison in much the same way Delaney and his friends had once talked about going upstate to college. "The young men spoke of it as a rite of passage," wrote Delaney, "and of choices they had made of going to Elmira to be with a cousin, Attica to be with an uncle, or Coxsackie to be with friends from the 'hood. The war on drugs that these men are adapting to can only come back to haunt all Americans."

This month, 8 million Americans will go jogging, 7 million will play tennis, and 6 million will do cocaine.

A few of those 6 million may be your patients.

You may have trouble recognizing cocaine abuse because there are few visible symptoms. Often the only way to find out is to ask the right questions.

Any cocaine use is potential *abuse*. Give your patients who have a problem the 1-800-COCAINE hotline or the National Institute on Drug Abuse information and referral line (1-800-662-HELP).

PARTNERSHIP FOR A DRUG-FREE AMERICA

deltakos USA

Healthcare Division
of J. Walter Thompson

JWT

RIGHTS VERSUS PROTECTION

Close your eyes. Now imagine a drug user. What does that person look like? When this question was part of a survey (the results of which were published in 1995 in the *Journal of Alcohol and Drug Education*), 95 percent of the people who responded pictured an African-American drug user, while only 5 percent imagined other racial groups. The truth is, however, that most drug users in the United States are white. And yet the nation's drug enforcement policies have affected more African Americans than any other group.

An African-American man who uses drugs is more likely to be arrested than a white man who uses the same drugs, and more likely to be convicted. Once convicted, he is likely to receive a more severe sentence. African Americans make up about 13 percent of the U.S. population and, studies show, 13 percent of America's drug users. But blacks constitute 35 percent of all people arrested for drug possession, 55 percent of those convicted for drug possession, and 74 percent of those sentenced to prison for drug possession. These percentages are the result of three overlapping trends:

1. Drug law enforcement is concentrated in inner cities, where more African Americans live.

2. African Americans who live in inner-city areas have fewer treatment programs available to them; as a result, drug abuse in these communities is more likely to be seen as a criminal justice problem rather than a social problem that needs intervention.

3. Mandatory sentencing laws impose harsher punishment for offenses involving crack cocaine than for offenses involving powder cocaine, and crack is favored by more African-American addicts than the more expensive powder cocaine.

This policy of treating crack abuse more severely is a controversial one. In 1986 federal laws created a 100-to-1 ratio between the amount of crack and powder cocaine needed to trigger mandatory sentences. In other words, an offender would receive a five-year sentence for the possession of 500 grams of powder cocaine, while another offender would receive the same sentence for only 5 grams of crack. Crack was also the only drug that carried a mandatory prison sentence for first-offense possession. Many people felt strongly both for and against these laws.

Those who wanted more severe punishments for crack crimes denied that their opinion had anything to do with race. Instead, they listed several other reasons why possessing this form of cocaine was a more serious offense than possessing powder cocaine. For instance, they noted that crack is more psychologically addictive, because it produces a quicker and more intense high than powder cocaine. The effects of crack also do not last as long as those of powder cocaine, meaning that the user will quickly require more. What's more, crack can be packaged in very small, cheap amounts, while powder cocaine cannot. This means that crack is more likely to be marketed to kids. Crack is usually sold in street markets and "crack houses," which means it makes a definite connection between a particular neighborhood and drug use. This connection leads to the deterioration of that community. In the end, insisted proponents of mandatory sentencing, more violent crime is associated with crack than with powder cocaine.

However, those who were against harsher mandatory sentences for crack possession had their own arguments. Crack and powder cocaine are merely two forms of the same drug, the way beer and whiskey are two forms of alcohol. A person possessing powder cocaine can easily turn it into crack—so why should powder cocaine possession warrant a lighter sentence than crack possession? People against mandatory sentencing also insisted that violence connected with crack use is actually rare. Alcohol, they pointed out, accounts for far more violent incidents than crack does. And, they added, most of the crime that involves crack is petty theft and prostitution. However, turf wars between Colombian and Cuban drug lords over powder cocaine in the late 1970s and 1980s led to thousands of murders.

In addition, prisons are filled with young African Americans serving mandatory sentences for crack crimes. Twenty-one percent of these are classified as "low level" security risks. (In other words, they have no record of violence, no involvement in more sophisticated criminal activities, and no prior prison experience.) Giving these offenders lighter sentences would save the federal government billions of dollars.

Is crack use really a more serious offense? Or do law enforcement and criminal justice officials perceive crack users to be more dangerous to society simply because these users are often black? The Clinton administration asked Congress to address this possible

Under mandatory sentencing laws, possession of only five grams of crack (created by heating powder cocaine) leads to a five-year prison sentence.

injustice, and in 1995 the U.S. Sentencing Commission also recommended to Congress that the 100-to-1 ratio be changed. However, Congress eventually rejected the proposal to revise the mandatory sentencing laws. In 1997, the Sentencing Commission again recommended that the difference between crack and powder cocaine sentences be reduced, but the law was not changed. In March 1999 the Crack-Cocaine Equitable Sentencing Act was introduced in Congress and later that month referred to a committee for review, where, as of March 2001, it remains.

Other drug laws, critics charge, also need to be changed. Suppose, for example, that a teenager threw a party for her friends while her parents were away for the weekend. The police got word of the party, and they heard a rumor that drugs were being used inside the

house. According to the laws relating to "probable cause"—which means the police had reason to believe a drug crime was being committed—they could not only arrest those who had attended the party, but they could also seize the property involved with the crime. In other words, based only on a rumor, the police could take the house. The guilt or innocence of the property owners—in this case, the teenager's parents—wouldn't matter, since the property itself was part of a drug crime.

According to the *Annual Report of the Department of Justice Asset Forfeiture Program*, between 1985 and 1991, the total value of assets seized by the federal government increased by more than 1,500 percent. In 1991 alone, the Department of Justice seized $643 million worth of property.

This money went into a fund supporting Department

Five hundred grams of powder cocaine triggers the same mandatory sentence as only five grams of crack.

of Justice programs, but some of the funds were returned to the local police departments that made the arrests, which might be viewed as a conflict of interest. Terrence Reed, a Washington, D.C., lawyer who was the American Bar Association's adviser to a drafting committee of the National Conference of Commissioners on Uniform State Laws regarding asset forfeiture, said that these cases had become a "cash cow" for law enforcement. The potential for abuse was just too great.

For this reason, the American Bar Association, the American Civil Liberties Union, and the National Association of Criminal Defense Lawyers all called for reform of asset forfeiture laws. The Justice Department resisted this reform, and many members of Congress feared that if they supported it they might be accused of being "soft on crime." However, two influential congressmen, Henry Hyde of Illinois and John Conyers of Michigan, supported bills that would place more restrictions on the seizure of property relating to drug crimes. Early in 2000, the Civil Asset Forfeiture Reform Act was passed. This act guarantees that:

- The government must first prove a "substantial connection between the property and the offense." In other words, a mere rumor will no longer be enough to justify the seizure of a car, a house, or any other property.
- The government must *tell* people before it seizes their property.
- It will be easier to get back the seized property. Free law counsel is provided to those who need it, and property owners no longer have to post a bond before trying to get their property back.
- Innocent owners—like the parents of drug-using teenagers—will be able to reclaim their property more easily.
- Owners who successfully sue for the return of their property will be compensated for damages and legal expenses.

Carol Thomas, of Millville, New Jersey, stands by her 1990 Ford Thunderbird, which was seized after her son was caught selling marijuana from it. A judge ordered the car returned to Thomas on January 19, 2001, but she is suing the state anyway, claiming that asset forfeiture laws are unconstitutional.

Although critics of American drug policies consider the Civil Asset Forfeiture Reform Act a step in the right direction, many continue to point to another contentious issue: drug searches.

In 1998, Gwendolyn Richards, a 27-year-old African-American woman, was returning to Chicago from Jamaica when a Customs Service inspector pulled her out of a line of air travelers. The inspector ordered

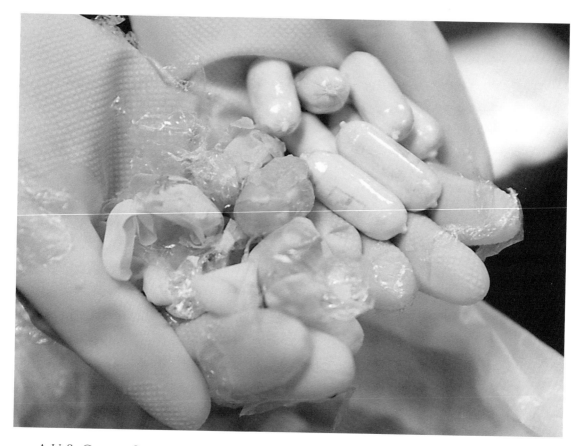

A U.S. Customs Service employee displays samples of seized condoms containing heroin, which were smuggled into the United States by people who swallowed the drug packages to avoid detection. U.S. courts are struggling to define the ways that Customs can search for drugs like these without infringing on the rights of innocent people.

Ms. Richards into a small room where she was strip-searched, X-rayed, and probed internally by a doctor. An armed guard then handcuffed Ms. Richards and led her through O'Hare International Airport; she was taken to a hospital for a drug search that lasted four hours. No drugs were ever found.

"I was humiliated. I couldn't believe it was happening," Ms. Richards told *Jet* magazine in the December 21, 1998, issue. "They had no reason to think I had drugs." She joined a class-action civil rights lawsuit brought by others against the Customs Service.

In 1998, a total of 2,447 searches similar to Ms. Richards's were conducted on airline passengers. Customs officials say such searches are necessary to catch drug smugglers who swallow cocaine-filled balloons, insert packages of cocaine into body cavities, or hide drugs in wooden legs or under the cover of false pregnancies. However, only 27 percent of those searched in 1998 were found to be carrying drugs. Approximately 60 percent of the people searched were African American or Hispanic.

Several complaints and lawsuits have caused Customs to review its policies and find less intrusive ways to search for drugs. The U.S. Constitution protects American citizens against unlawful search and seizure. The courts must decide when law enforcement agents violate citizens' civil liberties in waging America's War on Drugs.

For instance, in 1998, the Supreme Court unanimously ruled that a traffic violation (say, a speeding ticket) does not automatically give police the right to search the motorist's car for drugs. But the issue of illegal search comes up in other, less obvious, areas as well.

The question underlies the legality of mandatory drug testing in sports, schools, and jobs. In effect, drug testing is one of the most invasive forms of search, since it involves an individual's very body. The courts in general have maintained that drug testing is appropriate in jobs that affect public safety—like those held by train operators and employees who handle heavy machinery—where drug use could endanger human life. Likewise, in school sports, where the use of performance-enhancing drugs like steroids or "speed" (amphetamines) would be a form of cheating, according to the courts, mandatory testing is also acceptable. However, for public school activities like the chess club, chorus, drama club, or the debate team, routine testing has been found to be unconstitutional.

The laws that apply to money laundering are another controversial area in U.S. drug policy. Technically, any transfer of ill-gained funds (such as money from a drug deal), even depositing money in a bank, constitutes money laundering and could result in a long prison sentence. The standards have been so vague, claims James Bovard, author of *Freedom in Chains: The Rise of the State and the Demise of the Citizen,* that "anyone who has a one-time surge of income—such as selling a car or receiving a bonus at work—could be reported as a suspected drug dealer."

In December 1998, federal banking agencies proposed even tougher regulations for suspected money laundering. According to the new rules, banks must determine their customers' sources of funds; determine, understand, and monitor the normal and expected transactions of their customers; and report any customer transactions that are determined to be unusual or inconsistent with that customer's normal pattern.

These new regulations build upon existing Currency Transaction Reports that banks must file for any customer who makes a transaction involving $10,000 or more. No search warrant would be required before federal regulators looked at private financial records. Economists quoted in *Investors' Business Daily* fear that the new regulations will "take another step toward turning banks into undercover agents conspiring against the consumer." And James Bovard adds that these requirements are unwarranted searches of people's financial affairs; in effect, the regulations are an invasion of privacy. Furthermore, the new requirements will flood federal agencies with tons of paperwork; real crimes, Bovard warns, will be likely to go uncaught among the piles of unnecessary reports.

Most Americans agree that they want drug criminals caught, particularly the big-time drug dealers who may launder enormous sums of money. But at the same time, the public does not want to lose the rights guaranteed by the Constitution—rights like privacy, due process, and protection from unlawful search and seizure. The balance between ensuring our rights and protecting us from crime is a delicate one.

Unfortunately, the drug problem is not merely an

American dilemma, so it cannot be solved by American policies alone. Instead, drug use is a worldwide scourge. No matter how hard Americans try, they will not erase the drug problem from their communities unless they also deal with the problem's roots—and these roots lie outside the United States.

In order to recognize the extent of drug-related crime, we need to reach out beyond America's boundaries. We need to think globally.

INTERNATIONAL DRUG TRAFFICKING

In James Inciardi's book *The War on Drugs*, he includes a story told by a Miami drug dealer:

[T]he stuff [drugs] started out in a small lab . . . in north Laos up near the Chinese border. It made its way to Bangkok okay where it was supposed to be flown to Athens, Amsterdam, New York, and then to Miami by car. But . . . the guy who's supposed to make the transfer in Athens gets picked up for somethin' or other, so they fly it to Singapore instead. They had someone there who could take it most of the way . . . but he decides to get himself killed in Kuwait before he even gets there. So get this: It goes back to Bangkok, to somewhere in India, then somewhere else in the Middle East, and then up the Nile to Egypt. . . . Somehow it finds its way to South

Drug trafficking is an international problem. Here, a member of the Colombian police antidrug special forces discovers a cocaine laboratory where a ton of cocaine was being produced weekly. The weekly profits in American drug deals from this one lab amounted to $20 million.

Africa . . . and goes by ship to Uruguay, and then up through South America—Ecuador, Colombia, Peru, and all that— to Panama, Mexico City, Chicago, Detroit, New York, and then Miami.

Clearly, drugs reach America after traveling complicated routes that connect nations all around the world. Illegal drugs are a transnational problem.

Much of America's legitimate economy reaches across national borders as well. Since the middle of the 20th century, the earth's economic and social organizations have been changing enormously. Nations can no longer be considered totally separate, individual entities; instead, our world has become interconnected. Big corporations do their business around the world, dealing with the global economy rather than the financial conditions of just one nation.

The criminal narcotics industry is the illegal counterpart of lawful multinational corporations. From these legal conglomerates, the illegal drug trade learned the value of diversification; in other words, drug traffickers have branched out into other money-making schemes. In addition to drugs, these international traffickers deal in counterfeiting; terrorism; money laundering; child exploitation and pornography; prostitution; arms; mercenaries; biological, chemical, and nuclear materials; the black market sale of human organs for transplantation; and other outlaw enterprises. In an interdependent world where trade barriers are shrinking, drug money is also used to support various political causes. As a result, international politics may become intertwined with the movement of dangerous and illegal goods. Criminal drug rings may intermesh with legitimate businesses as well. Like a cancer that infects the world, illegal drugs have spread throughout the global systems, threatening our planet's physical and financial health.

During the days of slavery, a triangle of trade connected Africa (where human lives were the commodity being sold), the West Indies (where slaves were bought and rum was the product in demand), and America (where there was a market for both slaves and rum). Today drug trafficking routes have multiplied that simple triangle into numerous complex patterns of exchange.

For instance, Russian crime groups, operating in the United States and Puerto Rico, have formed coalitions with Colombian drug traffickers, exchanging weapons for cocaine. The drugs are mostly shipped to Europe, and the proceeds are laundered through offshore banks in the Caribbean. More than 30 such crime organizations operate out of Miami and New York, where they arrange arms-for-cocaine deals with partners in Russia.

Heroin reaches American streets through a complex web of production and trafficking networks that stretches all the way from Asia to the United States. Millions of peasant farmers are involved, as are tens of thousands of corrupt government officials, criminal businessmen, and street-level dealers.

Much of America's heroin comes from opium that is grown in Southeast Asia, in the hills of Burma (today called Myanmar), Thailand, and Laos. This area is referred to as the Golden Triangle, and in the late 1960s and early 1970s, it became the world's largest producer of illegal opium, growing as much as 700 metric tons (or 1.54 million pounds) each year.

In the 1970s, because of a combination of poor crops and law enforcement, the Golden Triangle did not produce as much opium as it once did. In the late '70s, another area in Asia began growing opium that was less expensive and generally more potent. This new area of production stretched across Southwest Asia through Pakistan, Iran, and Afghanistan; it became known as the Golden Crescent. By the mid-1980s, over half the heroin entering the United States came from here. Iran grew most of the opium, and Pakistan and Afghanistan refined it into heroin and shipped it on its way. By 1990, the combined opium from the Golden

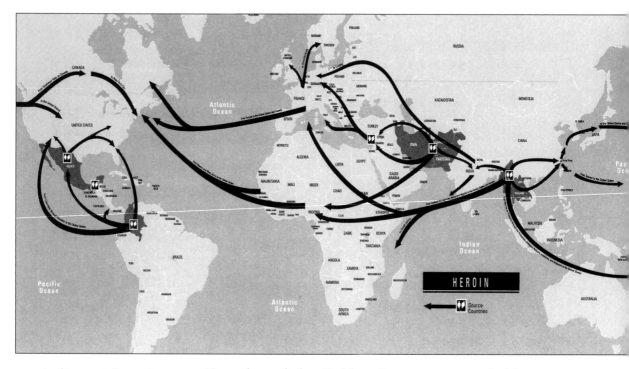

As this map indicates, heroin travels in a complicated web of routes connecting many countries around the world.

Triangle and the Golden Crescent was probably more than 1,500 metric tons.

Today, Burma in the Golden Triangle is once again one of the chief producers of opium. In 1997, approximately 2,600 metric tons of opium were shipped out of Burma, about 60 percent of the total amount the entire world uses. As of 1996, two-thirds of the heroin seized by law-enforcement agents on U.S. streets came from Burma.

Once opium is refined into heroin, it travels through a web of transportation routes, carriers, and payoffs. Depending on the individual crime organization's particular routes, the drug may be shipped through Indonesia, the Philippines, Syria, Egypt, Kenya, Nigeria, Italy, France, England, Germany, the Netherlands, Canada—or a combination of any of those nations. The numerous and complicated routes make it more difficult for law enforcement to break into the transportation system.

Many kinds of people carry heroin across the world and into the United States. Some are members of the crime organization, traveling alone or with their families as tourists. Others may be corrupt diplomats, pilots and other airline personnel, professional athletes, students, ship captains, doctors, or judges. Some drug traffickers even recruit attractive women to carry their drugs to American cities.

Once heroin is in the United States, it is diluted. What started out as pure heroin is cut with milk sugar, cornstarch, or almost any other powdery substance that will dissolve when heated. (Occasionally, heroin is mixed with cleaning powder or dirt—and even poisons like arsenic or strychnine.)

By the time heroin reaches the streets, its price has gone up astronomically. For instance, raw opium grown in Burma costs between $66 and $75 for one kilogram (2.2 pounds). By the time it reaches the Thailand border it sells for $900 to $1,000. The price for wholesale heroin in America leaps to $90,000 to $250,000 per kilo—and the street price for that same kilo runs between $400,000 and $940,000.

This extraordinary price markup means that the people along the drug routes are making enormous amounts of money. That's one reason why stamping out the drug trade is so difficult. Greed is a powerful motivator—and on a purely practical level, drug production and trafficking is tightly linked to some nations' economies. The peasant farmers who grow the opium may not be making the same sort of profits as those further along the drug route, but the farmers nevertheless depend on their crop for their families' livelihood.

Cocaine reaches the United States by another set of production and trafficking routes that begin in the Andes Mountains in South America. There peasant farmers grow the coca leaves, and then ship the leaves to refineries, where they are turned into coca paste, a kind of crude cocaine. Next, the coca paste goes to the Amazon River Valley, a tropical rain forest that covers 2.5 million square miles of Brazil, Peru, Colombia, Ecuador, Venezuela, Suriname, and Guyana. This land is close to cities and yet so densely forested that it is impossible for law enforcement to patrol. By means of many small and big deals, most of the coca paste works its way to Colombia, where it is refined into pure cocaine.

Cocaine plays an important part in Colombia's economy. At least 80 percent of the cocaine that enters the United States was grown as well as produced in Colombia. Drug traffickers give coca seed and fertilizer to peasants with the promise to buy the mature crop at two or three times the prices the farmers could make growing other products.

From Colombia, the cocaine goes by air or sea into the United States, taking so many routes that U.S. border officials cannot possibly block them all. As one Miami drug trafficker explained in Inciardi's book, "With the combination of good coordination, good connections, good navigation equipment, good navigation skills, plus a few payoffs here and there, coke can be safely brought in at any time."

Like heroin, cocaine is also mixed with other powders—milk sugar, baking soda, caffeine, quinine, lidocaine, powdered laxatives, or even borax. What started out as 500 kilograms of coca leaves worth about $4,000 to the grower is ultimately turned into 8 kilos of street cocaine worth about $500,000.

From cities like Miami, Chicago, Houston, Los Angeles, New York, Philadelphia, and San Francisco, gangs move the drug to other cities, towns, and rural areas. Gangs also change powder cocaine into crack. Most of the cocaine sold in the United States is converted into crack once it is inside American borders, and the market for crack drives the entire American cocaine trade. More than any other drug, crack has a devastating effect on the urban neighborhoods it infects.

Drug dealing is a big business that functions on many highly organized levels. For instance, one drug trafficking group, the Cali cartel, built illegal drug "cells" that operated in different geographic regions across the United States. Each cell was made up of 10 or more employees who knew little about the dealings of other cells. Within the individual cells, smaller units specialized in particular pieces of the illegal drug trade, such as cocaine storage, transportation, wholesale distribution, communications, or money laundering. Each unit reported to a cell manager, who in turn reported to a regional director. This person answered to one of the Cali leaders or their chief of operations in Colombia. This type of compartmentalization protected drug dealers from law enforcement. Since each unit worked independently of one another, if one drug dealer was arrested, he would not be able to give the police much information about the rest of the Cali group. However, the federal Drug Enforcement Administration has

Members of the Spanish National Police unload packages containing more than 19,000 pounds of cocaine. The cocaine, which was confiscated from a boat, will be burnt. In this case, a small portion of the drug trafficking web was intercepted and destroyed.

managed to dismantle many Cali drug cells working in the United States.

Drugs also enter the United States via Mexico. In 1997, customs officers intercepted 607,000 pounds of marijuana and 46,000 pounds of cocaine at the border between the United States and Mexico. Large quantities of heroin and methamphetamine also cross the border hidden in cars, trucks, and trains. Despite border patrols and searches conducted with X-ray machines or other high-tech equipment, so much commerce goes back and forth across the U.S.-Mexican border that inspecting all vehicles and people is virtually impossible. Furthermore, Mexican police and government officials have been found to be corrupt, sometimes using donations from drug dealers to fund their election campaigns. These officials may also have friends or relatives who are illegal drug traffickers.

Cooperation between the two countries—in terms of economic aid, training for law-enforcement officers, equipment for drug surveillance, and support for honest people—is the best approach for dealing with this extremely complex problem with one of America's closest neighbors. However, American intelligence experts warn that caution must be taken when working with Mexican authorities. Sensitive information (which could be used to catch drug dealers) could end up in the wrong hands.

Since drug trafficking is a global situation, it makes sense that drug dealing has also become a worldwide problem. Western Europe is now the second largest cocaine market in the world. Colombian drug traffickers have established relationships with Italian organized crime families (the Mafia), as well as Russian criminal groups and Spanish crime rings. The Iberian Peninsula (Spain and Portugal) now serves as the "gateway to Europe" for South American cocaine. Recently, more and more cocaine seems to also be entering Europe through the Netherlands, Belgium, France, Germany,

Italy, and England. Drug trafficking is increasing in Greece and Ireland as well because of the harbors and ports in both countries. Following the fall of the Soviet Union, the drug trade spread to Eastern Europe and other parts of Russia, where illegal crime syndicates have grown strong under the new, weaker governments. Although Jamaican groups sell crack to the United Kingdom's inner cities, the drug of choice for the rest of Europe seems to be powder cocaine.

Likewise, Australia now offers drug dealers a huge cocaine market. Colombian drug groups have also chosen this island nation as a good stepping-stone for shipping cocaine to Japan, where they are trying to promote cocaine use. So far, Japan is proving to be fairly resistant to illegal drugs.

A U.S. Customs enforcement officer searches a car for hidden drugs at the U.S.-Mexico border. Because there is so much profit to be made, high volumes of drugs continue to be smuggled into the United States regardless of attempts to tighten control at the borders.

Australian police arrest a suspect in an international drug ring that included residents of Hong Kong and Indonesia. The illegal drug trade crosses a multitude of national borders, greatly complicating law-enforcement efforts.

In Africa, however, a number of countries have experienced a surge in cocaine abuse. Ghana, Nigeria, and South Africa all have their share of problems with this drug, as do nations in northern Africa like Algeria, Morocco, and Tunisia.

In the Middle East, Lebanon is now a center for dealing as well as processing cocaine. In 1996, government authorities intercepted 166 kilograms of cocaine, up from only 13.6 kilograms the year before. The intercepted drugs were found hidden in shipments of wooden doors, ceramic tiles, and even food. Approximately 80 percent of the cocaine brought into Lebanon is exported through Jordan and Syria to Europe or markets in the Persian Gulf, but the rest remains in the area to be used by the residents of the country.

Contact points for illegal drugs can change rapidly and frequently because of the following characteristics of the modern world:

- worldwide electronic banking;
- a variety of air, sea, and overland transportation systems;
- different law-enforcement structures from country to country;
- respect for national sovereignty;
- instant communication through telephone, fax, E-mail, and the Internet; and
- the complexities of international money exchange.

For instance, when laws are passed discouraging money laundering in one nation, funds can easily flow to another country instead. If illegal arms are suddenly sought on another continent, the drug trade easily accommodates the switch in products.

As long as people want to buy illegal drugs and so much money can be made providing them, criminals will continue to find ways to smuggle drugs into the United States. When police tighten patrols along the Mexican border, for example, more drugs start coming through the Caribbean route on boats and planes. Drugs are an international problem that has become intertwined with regional economies and conflicts. As a result, whether directly or indirectly, drugs are implicated in the murder of hundreds of innocent people.

In 1976, Pablo Escobar was arrested for selling cocaine. Escobar belonged to the powerful Medellín cartel. Soon after his arrest, the police officers who had apprehended him were murdered. Next, one judge after another declined to hear the case until all records of the crime mysteriously disappeared.

Americans realized that Colombia's corruption and violence had followed cocaine across Florida's borders. By 1980, Florida's illegal drug trade had become a $7 billion business, outstripping the Sunshine State's next largest industry—tourism—by $5 billion.

This terrifying achievement was accomplished by way of the Colombian drug traffickers' violent methods.

Today, Colombian drug cartels control much of the worldwide traffic in illegal substances, and ruthlessness continues to be their hallmark. Massacres committed by Colombian drug dealers often extend to family, friends, and even pets associated with the victims. Savage and gruesome acts are intended to terrify rival dealers. Law-enforcement officials who try to resist these drug criminals are sometimes given a choice between "silver or lead," meaning bribes or bullets. Dealers make phone threats, mentioning the names of parents, children, or wives to the individuals they are intimidating. A severed cow tongue might be delivered to the person's home, or strong men may follow the victim throughout the day. Rivals and their families and friends are often murdered.

Even though many of the top Colombian drug traffickers have been taken into police custody, such arrests sometimes merely mean that other competing drug groups have gotten the upper hand. In addition, drug lords have been known to conduct illegal enterprises from behind bars. *The Economist* recently ran a piece claiming that Cali cartel leaders in Colombia "have been running their drug business from the comfort of their prison cells." The article describes brutal murders within the prison and speculates that rival drug dealers were responsible for the killings.

For instance, on November 5, 1999, a well-dressed man posing as a lawyer strolled into the Palmira maximum-security prison near Cali. He warmly embraced Helmer "Pacho" Herrera—a top dog in the Cali mob— then shot him six times in the head. Eight days later, Orlando Henao Montoya—the head of the Valle cartel, Cali's onetime ally—was gunned down in another maximum-security prison. This time, it was Pacho Herrera's paraplegic brother who fired the shots from his electric wheelchair.

In Colombia itself, the home of these violent groups, this sort of violence is all too common. In one year, 17 police officers, 4 judges, and many businessmen were murdered, while 11 other judges received death threats. At one point, 180 frightened magistrates and judges resigned at once. Democracy and the rule of law withered in the face of such violence. The United States provides aid to Colombia for antidrug efforts. But the political situation in that country is complicated by a long-running guerrilla war, and the insurgents and drug traffickers have worked together to advance their respective goals.

One thing is certain: nations around the world must work together if they are to fight the drug problem that has spread around the globe. This sort of international cooperation is difficult but not impossible.

A Look at
the Future

Ⅰn the first half of the 20th century, 10 to 15 million people came down with smallpox every year; one out of three people who caught smallpox died. But in 1953, the World Health Organization (WHO) asked that everywhere around the world children be immunized against this disease. Persuading the entire globe to work together was not easy, but after 13 years earth's nations agreed to WHO's proposal. Around the world children were vaccinated for smallpox, and doctors worked together to contain the disease. In 1980, WHO determined that smallpox had been completely wiped out. This deadly disease was conquered because the world united to achieve a common goal.

Following a similar model, the international community could unite to confront the drug problem. And in fact, the world's nations have been trying to do

Members of the United Nations meet to plan ways to work together toward a drug-free future around the world.

As this antidrug poster in Beijing, China, demonstrates, nations around the world are working to educate young people about the dangers of drugs. Prevention and education may be the only practical way to reduce drug use internationally.

just that. The United Nations and other organizations have drafted convention agreements and passed strategies for combating the international drug problem. Together, nations have developed model legislation against drug crimes, as well as a system of data collection for supply-and-demand statistics. They have sponsored expert seminars on a range of drug issues, and they have worked out a mutual legal assistance agreement with regional standing so that countries could cooperate in prosecuting drug criminals who operate in more than one nation. One international organization also helps with legal action against the international drug trade. It hopes to build a judicial center in Latin America to train judges and court personnel, as well as promote the rule of law and democracy. This would be an important addition to worldwide antidrug efforts.

Furthermore, the U.N. Special Session on Narcotics recently prepared a declaration on the importance of demand reduction, since prevention and education are essential in reducing drug use internationally. Treatment for the chemically dependent, both inside correctional facilities and within society at large, is the only way to break the cycle of drugs and crime that plagues the streets of so many cities around the world.

All these alliances and plans are hopeful signs that the world is coming together to tackle the problem of drug abuse. Unfortunately, there is often a gap between what is said in legislation or agreements and what actually takes place on an international level. Working out the details is a difficult challenge—but practical actions are being taken against drugs.

Throughout the late 1990s, the United States, Colombia, and Peru have targeted drug-laden aircraft flying between coca-growing regions of Peru and pro-cessing laboratories in Colombia. At the same time a project has been put into effect that provides financial alternatives to coca farmers; these poor peasants are paid to grow other produce that would otherwise be less lucrative than drug crops. As a result of these two campaigns, coca cultivation in Peru—once the source of more than half the world's cocaine—has decreased by 40 percent.

The United States also funded the same sort of alternative crop programs in Bolivia, and these rein-forced the Bolivians' own coca-control efforts in the Chaparé region. Potential cocaine production declined 13 percent in Bolivia as a result. The amount of land devoted to legal crops in the Chaparé is now 127 percent greater than it was in 1986.

Unfortunately, progress in Bolivia and Peru over the past years has been offset by a 56 percent expansion of coca farming in Colombia. Guerrilla and paramili-tary forces control these areas where coca is grown. The United States has tried to control the cocaine problem on an agricultural level by paying Colombian pilots to spray poison from the air on coca plants. Almost 99,000 acres of coca were destroyed in this way. The United States increased the amount of money donated to Colombia for fighting illegal drugs from $22 million to $100 million. Because of these efforts, Colombian authorities have been able to arrest seven top drug traffickers.

The United States plans to expand its support of the Colombian attack against drug growing. Americans will help police Colombia's rivers and ports, while at the same time working to strengthen alternative crop development programs. The Unites States will also provide training and equipment to judicial systems, law-enforcement agencies, and security forces. Meanwhile, the U.S. government is encouraging the Colombians to cooperate with all these efforts.

Unfortunately, experts face a growing realization that reducing the drug supply to users is a strategy doomed to failure. Shortfalls in one part of a country or the world are easily offset by greater production elsewhere. As long as there is significant demand for illegal drugs and huge profits to be made, an ample supply of illegal drugs are produced one place or another to satisfy this market. Reducing the demand for illegal drugs through education, treatment, and law enforcement appears to be a far more effective approach. This policy will need to be pursued internationally, however, before the world will see results.

Money laundering is another area where international agreements can be effective if enforced. Billions of dollars in illegal profits from drugs must be converted into legal accounts ("laundered") if such funds are to go undetected. In the United States alone, drug trafficking organizations seek to launder $57 billion a year. The Department of the Treasury works with U.S. banks, wire transmitters, vendors of money orders and travelers checks, and other financial services to prevent transfers of drug proceeds. The federal government uses provisions of the Bank Secrecy Act to detect suspicious transactions. Although we have already seen that Americans do not want money-laundering laws to invade the privacy of law-abiding citizens, at the worldwide level, money laundering remains a serious problem. Because the problem by its very nature reaches across borders (the best way to hide illegal money is often to transfer it to a foreign bank account), it must be attacked at an international level.

Twenty-six nations belong to the Financial Action Task Force, which develops international anti-money-laundering standards. Under the International Economic

Emergency Powers Act, the United States alone has imposed sanctions against more than 400 businesses affiliated with Colombian criminal drug operations. American experts have also helped draft regulations to protect financial sectors in other countries.

The General Assembly of the United Nations, in a Special Session on Narcotics, issued a declaration condemning money laundering. However, more often than not, concrete action hasn't followed all the talk. Countries like Panama need to realize that preventing money laundering, which burdens legitimate business and saps economic health, is in their long-term interest. In the modern world of international banking, the

Soldiers of the Colombian army guard two injured members of a rebel group. The rebel fighters were wounded during an attack protesting President Clinton's visit to Colombia. Clinton was delivering an aid package as part of America's support of Colombia's antidrug campaign.

transfer of money electronically from country to country has become easy and widespread. As long as some countries continue to allow illegal money to be transferred into their banks, money laundering will continue. Worldwide compliance with money-laundering regulations is essential for the credibility of financial institutions competing in a global economy.

Nations can also attack the drug trade by seizing illegally gained assets. The U.S. Department of Justice (DOJ) assisted in drafting asset-forfeiture legislation in Bermuda, Bolivia, Brazil, Colombia, Mexico, South Africa, and Uruguay. The DOJ also coordinated international forfeiture cases in Austria, Britain, Luxembourg, and Switzerland, among other countries. As discussed in an earlier chapter, however, one problem connected with this practice is that assets sometimes have been confiscated from defendants who have been charged with drug crimes but not convicted. The police departments' desire to profit from properties connected with drug crime can lead to corruption of the justice system or to improper arrests. This problem is particularly severe in nations where members of the police force and other government officials are corrupt.

When a person commits a crime in one country and then flees to another, that person can escape punishment unless the two countries have an agreement to return fugitives to face trial in the nation in which they are wanted. Such an agreement is called an extradition treaty. The United States has participated in more than 100 extradition treaties; in 1997 alone America signed another 17 new extradition treaties. As a result, extradition requests are becoming more frequent. In 1996, the U.S. government sought the extradition of 2,894 criminals, up from 1,672 in 1990.

Sharing intelligence information also makes international control of illegal drugs easier. While organizations like the National Drug Intelligence Center (NDIC), Treasury's Financial Center (FINCEN), and the El Paso

Intelligence Center (EPIC) are doing a good job at working together internationally, their full potential has yet to be realized. When countries like Mexico are increasingly controlled by organized crime, the danger in sharing intelligence is that information can fall into the wrong hands. America must decide wisely as to when and where cooperation is safe and effective.

The annual process of certifying the counterdrug performance of narcotics-producing and transit countries is another instrument for encouraging international cooperation. According to this process, the U.S. president reviews the counterdrug activities of different nations and determines whether they have cooperated with the United States or taken adequate steps on their own to meet the guidelines of the U.N. Convention Against Illicit Traffic in Narcotic Drugs and Psychotropic Substances. Denial of certification means that the financial assistance America sends to these countries will be cut; it also means that the United States will

Colombian police escort an accused drug lord to a plane bound for Florida, where he will face money laundering and cocaine trafficking charges. International extradition treaties are a potent weapon in the fight against drug traffickers.

vote against loans to such countries by international development banks.

Illegal drugs can also be addressed within the context of arms control and the management of other activities that threaten the earth's physical and social environment—like the sale of nuclear materials, the dumping of hazardous waste, biochemical sources of disease, counterfeiting, child pornography, prostitution, and a host of other dangerous products.

In 1996, the Organization of American States adopted an anticorruption convention—the first international agreement of its kind—to combat bribery, illegal enrichment, and related crimes. Likewise, in November 1999, President Clinton and President Ernesto Zedillo of Mexico signed a new hemispheric convention against illegal arms production and trafficking, which will help track the flow of illegal firearms, explosives, and ammunition. Illicit drug trade does not take place in a vacuum, and it could be controlled more effectively by targeting the conglomerate of other illegal activities with which it is enmeshed.

In the future, international regulatory bodies will need to work together. For instance, civil aviation might unite to keep out prohibited cargo (like drugs) and sanction violators. A world court to try international drug traffickers could rescue weak nations whose judicial systems are not strong enough to withstand threats and other pressures brought by criminal drug syndicates. Just as the Nuremberg Court prosecuted crimes against humanity in the genocide perpetrated by Nazi Germany, a world court could condemn international crime that harms nations around the world.

But while the United States needs to cooperate with all these international efforts, America also needs to continue its own efforts against drug use at home. The illegal drug business is larger than the oil and gas industry. It's twice as big as the motor vehicle industry. And while drugs make dealers rich, they make the United

States poorer. If left unchecked, illegal drugs will cost the United States $700 billion over the next 10 years—and 100,000 people will die because of drugs and drug-related crime. The cost is too high.

Illegal drugs rob Americans of their health; they also steal financial resources that the nation could spend on other priorities, such as education and health care. "Substance abuse is Public Health Enemy Number One in America," concluded Columbia University's four-year report on the cost of addiction. "The grim reality, shrouded for so long in our individual and national self-denial, is that any health reform that hopes to offer care to all Americans at a reasonable cost must mount an all-fronts attack on all substance abuse—legal and illegal drugs, alcohol and nicotine." Americans must face the facts: drugs are a big problem.

So how do we solve this problem? America's War on Drugs has gained some victories—but unfortunately, it has also suffered many defeats. The War on Drugs policies emphasize punishment over treatment. These policies hurt low-income communities and minority groups and have contributed to the enormous growth of the U.S. prison system over the last 20 years.

Barry McCaffrey, formerly the director of the Office of National Drug Control Policy under the Clinton administration, insists that we need to replace the War on Drugs concept with a new approach toward the drug problem. Drug users are not our enemies; they are a part of our communities. And we don't make war on our families, friends, relatives, and colleagues. Instead, we work with them to overcome their problems. Besides, wars last for a limited amount of time and come to a definite end—while the campaign to teach people to resist substance abuse is an unending task that must be relearned from generation to generation.

After looking at a series of studies, the Sentencing Project concluded that drug treatment is a more cost-effective way to control drug abuse and crime than is

These elementary students are participating in an antidrug march. Educating children about the dangers of drugs will, it is hoped, reduce drug abuse later on.

relying on harsh prison sentences to deter and contain drug users. The studies indicated that if America spent $1 million to expand the prison system, it would only reduce national drug use by 13 kilograms; but if the United States spent the same amount on treatment, it would do eight times as much good. The studies also estimated that treatment was 15 times more effective than mandatory sentencing at reducing drug crimes.

The Sentencing Project suggests that policymakers follow through on a number of proposed changes to America's drug policies. First, there should be a fundamental shift in funding priorities, from law enforcement to prevention and treatment. Next, the Sentencing Project recommends modifying mandatory sentencing laws, so that judges can consider the individual drug user and the unique circumstances of his or her case. An increase in treatment options within the criminal justice system is also strongly suggested, the belief being that if there were more funds to give people on parole or probation much-needed support, these people would be less likely to commit more drug-related crimes. The Sentencing Project has also proposed more funding for courts to assess offenders more efficiently, so that wise and effective sentencing options can be determined. And finally, a new view of drug abuse is required, the Sentencing Project concludes. Drug abuse should be seen as a community problem rather than merely a criminal issue, because people with low incomes have fewer treatment options available to them, so they are more apt to end up in the criminal justice system. But the criminal justice system was never designed to act as a social services agency, and if funding was available, low-income drug users would not have to wait to be arrested before they could apply for treatment.

Policymakers are taking steps to improve America's antidrug strategy. For instance, today the number-one goal of the National Drug Control Strategy is to help young people reject illegal drugs. Congress set aside $195 million for an antidrug media campaign aimed at young people, and the media matched that amount with free airtime for antidrug commercials. An entertainment initiative led by the Clinton White House has helped Hollywood understand the need for accurate depictions of drug abuse on TV and radio, in movies, and in other electronic media. These more realistic portrayals of drug use, it is hoped, will help children and young adults realize that addiction is neither normal nor glamorous. Meanwhile, treatment programs inside and outside prisons are being expanded. The government understands that the best way to prevent drug abuse is through education, combined with treatment.

Illegal drugs *are* a big problem. But if we give up hope, we will do nothing. By the same token, we will be less effective if we aim too high. Wiping out all drug abuse is not a realistic goal—but we can reduce the amount of abuse. If we work together, we can build a better and safer world.

Further Reading

Beschner, George, and Alfred S. Friedman. *Teen Drug Use*. Lexington, Mass.: Lexington Books, 1995.

Caulkins, J. P., et al. *Mandatory Minimum Drug Sentences: Throwing Away the Key or the Taxpayers' Money?* Santa Monica, Calif.: Rand Corporation, 1997.

Dupont, Robert. *The Selfish Brain: Learning from Addiction*. Washington, D.C.: American Psychiatric Press, 1997.

Elliott, Kimberly Ann. *Corruption and the Global Economy*. Washington, D.C.: Institute for International Economics, 1997.

Finn, Peter. *Miami's "Drug Court": A Different Approach*. Washington, D.C.: U.S. Department of Justice, 1993.

Friman, Richard. *NarcoDiplomacy: Exporting the U.S. War on Drugs*. Ithaca, N.Y.: Cornell University Press, 1996.

Goldstein, Avram. *Addiction: From Biology to Drug Policy*. New York: W. H. Freeman and Company, 1994.

Inciardi, James. *The War on Drugs: Heroin, Cocaine, Crime, and Public Policy*. Palo Alto, Calif.: Mayfield Publishing, 1986.

Jonnes, Jill. *Hep Cats, Narcs, and Pipe-Dreams: A History of America's Romance with Illegal Drugs*. New York: Scribner, 1996.

Kiev, Ari. *The Drug Epidemic*. New York: Macmillan, 1990.

Langrod, John, et al. *Substance Abuse: A Comprehensive Textbook* (3rd ed.). Baltimore: Williams & Wilkins, 1997.

Langton, Phyllis. *The Social World of Drugs*. Minneapolis–St. Paul: West Publishing Company, 1996.

Leons, Madeline Barbara, and Harry Sanabria, eds. *Coca, Cocaine, and the Bolivian Reality*. Albany: State University of New York Press, 1997.

Musto, David. *The American Disease: Origins of Narcotic Control*. New Haven, Conn.: Yale University Press, 1987.

Scott, Peter Dale, and Jonathan Marshall. *Cocaine Politics: Drugs, Armies, and the CIA in Central America*. Los Angeles: University of California Press, 1991.

Siegel, Ronald. *Intoxication: Life in Pursuit of Artificial Paradise*. New York: E. P. Dutton, 1989.

Sifakis, Carl. *Encyclopedia of American Crime*. New York: Facts on File, Inc., 1982.

Stares, Paul. *Global Habit: The Drug Problem in a Borderless World*. Washington, D.C.: Brookings Institute, 1996.

Trebach, Arnold S., and James A. Inciardi. *Legalize It? Debating America's Drug Policy*. Washington, D.C.: American University Press, 1993.

Walker, William, ed. *Drugs in the Western Hemisphere: An Odyssey of Cultures in Conflict*. Wilmington, Del.: Scholarly Resources, Inc., 1996.

Index

Adams, Samuel Hopkins, 25
Addiction, 17
African Americans, and criminal justice, 69-70, 71
Alcohol, 71
    illegal use of, 28-29
    legal use of, 26
Amphetamines, 38, 39
Anslinger, Harry J., 30
Asset forfeiture laws
    and international policy, 100
    and U.S. drug policy, 72-75

Barbiturates, 38, 39
Bayer and Company, 24-25
Beatles, the, 34
Belushi, John, 14
Bias, Len, 41
Bolivia, and cocaine, 97
Bush, George, 42

Caffeine, 26
Cali cartel (Colombia), 87-88, 92
Cannabis, 30
    See also Marijuana
Civil Asset Forfeiture Reform Act, 74-75
Clinton, Bill, 42-43, 62, 71, 102, 103, 105
Coca-Cola, and cocaine, 22-23, 26
Cocaine, 16
    and Coca-Cola, 22-23, 26
    and Colombia, 71, 86, 87-88, 89, 91-93, 97-98, 99
    crimes connected with, 49
    drug policy on, 26-27, 30

and drug trafficking, 88-90
as health risk, 13-14, 41
with heroin, 48
legal use of, 22-24, 29-30
price of, 86
in prisons, 65-66
reducing supply of, 97-98
teen use of, 18
    See also Crack
Codeine, 24
Colombia
    and drug trafficking, 71, 86, 87-88, 89, 91-93, 97
    fighting illegal drugs in, 97-98
    and money laundering, 99
Crack, 41-42
    and drug trafficking, 86
    punishments for, 70-72
Crack-Cocaine Equitable Sentencing Act, 72
Crime
    and alcohol use, 28-29
    and drug use, 18-19, 25, 27-28, 31, 42, 43, 45-49, 59
    See also Criminal justice; Drug policy
Criminal justice, 18, 30, 42, 43, 51-59
    and African Americans, 69-70, 71
    and arrest of drug users, 49, 51
    and asset forfeiture, 72-75
    and crack, 70-72
    and death penalty, 42

and drug courts, 57-58
and drug policy, 51-59, 53
and drug searches, 75-77
and drug testing, 77
and exclusionary rule, 42
and future, 103-105
and mandatory sentencing, 51-57, 70-72, 104
and money laundering, 77-78, 98-99
and penalties for drug use, 42, 52-53.
and treatment options, 104-105
and violation of drug laws, 42
    See also Prisons

Diacetylmorphine, 24
    See also Heroin
Drug courts, 57-58
Drug Enforcement Administration (DEA), 15-16, 40-41, 87-88
Drug-Free Prison Zone Demonstration Project, 66
Drug-Free Workplace, 42
Drug policy, 37-43
    and cost of illegal drugs, 103
    and dangers of drug use, 14
    and drug-crime connection, 48
    and future, 102-105
    history of, 26-31
    and illegality of drugs, 13-19
    and legal use of drugs, 42

and War on Drugs, 38,
  48, 53, 77, 103
and Weed and Seed
  program, 42
See also Criminal justice;
  Education; Treatment
  programs
Drugs
  as community problem,
    105
  dangers of, 13-19
  as ghetto problem, 33
  history of, in America,
    21-31
  legal use of, 21-26, 31,
    40, 42
  and 1960s, 34-36
  teen use of, 15-17, 18, 105
  and usage trends, 14-17
  widespread use of, 33-37
Drug searches, 75-77
Drug testing, 77
Drug trafficking, 40, 43,
  81-93
  and cocaine, 85-86, 88-90
  and Colombia, 86, 87-88,
    89, 91-93, 97
  and contact points, 91
  and diversification, 82
  efforts against, 27-28,
    95-102
  as global situation, 88-90
  and heroin, 83-85, 88
  history of, 27-28, 30-31
  and Mexico, 88
  and money laundering,
    98-100
  routes of, 83-86
  and violence, 91-93
Dylan, Bob, 34

Education
  and international drug
    use, 96, 98
  and U.S. drug policy, 14,
    53, 59, 105
18th Amendment, 28
Elders, Joycelyn, 42
Extradition treaties, 100

Federal Bureau of Investigation, 41
Federal Bureau of Prisons,
  64, 66
Florida, and illegal drug
  trade, 91-92
Ford, Gerald, 38

Golden Crescent, 83-84
Golden Triangle, 83-84

Hague Convention, 28
Harding, Warren, 28-29
Harrison Act, 26-27, 30
Hashish, 30
  See also Marijuana
Hemp, 41
Hendrix, Jimi, 14, 37
Heroin, 16
  with cocaine, 48
  crimes connected with,
    48, 49
  development of, 24-25
  drug policy on, 30, 37,
    38, 40
  and drug trafficking,
    83-85, 88
  legal use of, 19, 24-25,
    27, 28, 34
  price of, 46, 85
  purity of, 15

and 1960s, 34
Hoffman, Albert, 34-35

Intelligence information,
  worldwide sharing of,
  100-101
International community,
  efforts against drugs in,
  95-102
  alliances, 96-97
  extradition treaties, 100
  and money laundering,
    98-100
  and physical and social
    environment, 102
  reducing drug supply, 97-98
  reviewing counterdrug
    activities of countries,
    101-102
  sharing intelligence
    information, 100-101
  See also Drug trafficking
International Conference on
  Opium, 28
International Economic Emergency Powers Act, 98-99
International Foundation for
  Internal Freedom, 35

Jones-Miller Act, 28
Joplin, Janis, 14, 37
Jungle, The (Sinclair), 26

Leary, Timothy, 35-36
Lincoln, Abraham, 23
Linkletter, Art, 37
LSD, 34-37, 38

Mandatory sentencing,
  51-57, 70-72, 104

Index

Marijuana
    drug policy on, 30, 37, 38, 40, 41
    and drug trafficking, 88
    legal use of, 26, 34
    in prisons, 65-66
    and 1960s, 34
    teen use of, 15-16, 18
    THC in, 15
Marijuana Tax Act, 30
McCaffrey, Barry, 42-43, 103
Medellín cartel (Colombia), 91
Media, and antidrug campaign, 105
Methamphetamines, 16, 88
Methaqualone. See Quaalude
Mexico
    and antidrug efforts, 101, 102
    and drug trafficking, 88
Money laundering
    international efforts against, 98-100
    and U.S. drug policy, 77-78, 98-99
Morphine, 22, 25
Motion picture industry, and cocaine, 29-30

National Center on Addiction and Substance Use, 15-16
National Drug Control Strategy, 105
National Institute of Corrections, 66
National Institute of Justice, 48

National Institute on Drug Abuse, 48
National Organization for the Reform of Marijuana Laws, 40
Nicotine, 26
Nixon, Richard, 38, 48

Office of National Drug Control Policy, 17, 18, 42, 66
Operation Intercept, 37
Opium
    drug policy on, 26-27, 28
    and drug trafficking, 83-85
    legal use of, 21-22
    See also Heroin; Morphine
Organization of American States, 102

Pemberton, John, 22-23
Peru, and cocaine, 97
Presley, Elvis, 14
Prisons, 18, 30, 42, 51, 53, 59, 61-67
    cost of, 63-64
    drug treatment versus, 103-104
    drug use in, 65-67
    and inmate attitudes, 67
    and mandatory sentencing, 51-57
    treatment programs in, 62-65, 105
    and War on Drugs, 103
Probable cause, 72-73
Prohibition, 28-29
Psychedelic drugs, 34-37
Pure Food and Drug Act, 26

Quaalude, 39

Rand Drug Policy Research Center, 55-56
Reagan, Ronald, 41, 53
Rockefeller Drug Laws, 40
Rogers, Don, 41
Roosevelt, Theodore, 27-28
Rorer, William H., 39

Sentencing Project, the, 61, 65, 103-105
Sinclair, Upton, 26
Speakeasies, 28
Substance Abuse and Mental Health Services Administration, 18

Tobacco, 26
Treatment programs, 30, 37, 43, 53, 105
    and drug courts, 57-58
    effectiveness of, 103-104
    and international drug use, 96, 98
    mandatory sentencing versus, 56
    in prisons, 62-65, 105

United Nations, 96, 99
U.S. Sentencing Commission, 57, 72

Vietnam War, 34

War on Drugs, 38, 48, 53, 77, 103
Weed and Seed program, 42
Woodstock, New York, 34

Zedillo, Ernesto, 102

Picture Credits

page

2-3: Douglas C. Pizac/AP/Wide World Photos
12: Roger Ressmeyer/Corbis
15: Corbis Images MED2070
16: New Millennium Images
19: PhotoDisc Vol.25 #25223
20: Kamal Hyder/Newsmakers
23: New Millennium Images
24: Courtesy National Library of Medicine
25: Courtesy Drug Enforcement Administration
27: Library of Congress
29: New Millennium Images
31: New Millennium Images
33: Erika Larsen
35: Dan Callister/Newsmakers
36: AP/Wide World Photos
40: New Millennium Images

41: New Millennium Images
43: Tim Sloan/Agence France Presse
44: PhotoDisc Vol.25 #25215
47: Tom Mihalek/Newsmakers
50: AP/Wide World Photos
52: New Millennium Images
55: New Millennium Images
56: PRNews Photo/NMI
59: Rich Pedroncelli/AP/Wide World Photos
60: Brian C. Philips/Reuters
63: New Millennium Images
65: Ed Carreon/Zuma Press
68: Courtesy National Library of Medicine
72: Courtesy Drug Enforcement Administration
73: Courtesy Drug Enforcement Administration

75: Donna Connor/AP/Wide World Photos
76: Frances M. Robert/ Newsmakers
80-81: Piero Pomponi/Newsmakers
84: Courtesy Drug Enforcement Administration
87: Elvira Urquijo/Agence France Presse
89: Joe Raedle/Newsmakers
90: Agence France Presse
94-95: New Millennium Images
96: Goi Chai Hin/Agence France Presse
99: Jair Cabal/Agence France Presse
101: Jose Miguel Gomez/Reuters
104: AP/Wide World Photos

LINDA BAYER has a M.A. in psychology and studied for an Ed.D. at the Graduate School of Education at Harvard University. She also has an M.A. in English and a Ph.D. in humanities. Dr. Bayer worked with patients suffering from substance abuse and other problems at Judge Baker Guidance Center and within the Boston public school system. She served on the faculties of several universities, including Boston University and the Hebrew University in Israel, where she occupied the Sam and Ayala Zacks Chair and was twice a writer in residence in Jerusalem.

Dr. Bayer was a newspaper editor and syndicated columnist, winning a Simon Rockower Award for excellence in journalism. She is the author of hundreds of articles and is working on her 15th book. She has written for a number of public figures, including General Colin Powell and President Bill Clinton.

Dr. Bayer is the mother of two children, Lev and Ilana.

AUSTIN SARAT is William Nelson Cromwell Professor of Jurisprudence and Political Science at Amherst College, where he also chairs the Department of Law, Jurisprudence and Social Thought. Professor Sarat is the author or editor of 23 books and numerous scholarly articles. Among his books are *Law's Violence, Sitting in Judgment: Sentencing the White Collar Criminal,* and *Justice and Injustice in Law and Legal Theory.* He has received many academic awards and held several prestigious fellowships. He is President of the Law & Society Association and Chair of the Working Group on Law, Culture and the Humanities. In addition, he is a nationally recognized teacher and educator whose teaching has been featured in the *New York Times,* on the *Today* show, and on National Public Radio's *Fresh Air.*